NADIYA HUSSAIN

Nadiya's
BRITISH
FOOD
ADVENTURE

Photography by Chris Terry

MICHAEL JOSEPH
an imprint of
PENGUIN BOOKS

I dedicate this book to my grandparents – Dada, Dadi, Nana and Nani – who made sacrifices we will never truly understand or appreciate. They gave up their lives, their quiet hopes, their silent dreams and their loved ones to give us what we have today. Thanks to them we can say we are children of the world, and can see with our own eyes the world they only ever dreamed of seeing.

CONTENTS

INTRODUCTION

As a first-generation Brit, born to Bangladeshi immigrant parents, I grew up in a household where family was not just your mother, father and siblings, but also the grandparents, uncles, aunts, cousins, first-, second-, third-, fourth-cousins and even the neighbours. Everyone was family. If you knew us – or knew our father – you were family. It was an open-door policy in our home. If my parents were cooking and the smell wafted out of the kitchen window, then you were welcome.

For me growing up, the food I ate was the only food I knew of. Forget shopping lists, or menus, or special events – food for us was the excitement my dad felt when he walked through the door with a freshly bought tiger fish on his shoulder. It cost him a week's wages but it reminded him of home. In our family, Dad was the daydreamer.

For me growing up, food was about my mother sitting on the floor with her sisters-in-law, parcelling samosas, heavy work for one day making light work for the month, thirsty work equalling thrifty work. In our family, Mum was the workforce.

For me growing up, food was about visiting my sick brother in hospital and watching him sip a dense, murky cocoa drink to build up his strength while the rest of us ate fish and chips at the end of his hospital bed. Him watching us with sad eyes, desperate to eat real food, dreaming of mum's chicken and cabbage curry. Similarly, it was watching my poorly sister come round from her anaesthetic and knowing she craved the sweet taste of the fruit squash she wasn't allowed, while we sat by her bedside quenching our own thirst with flat, sugary Lucozade. The bitter with the sweet. She waited weeks to enjoy a spoonful of our sweet, scented vermicelli for breakfast. My brother and sister were the cravers of comfort and home.

The rest of us were lucky. Lucky to be at home, lucky to be able to eat whatever my nan cooked while my parents sat by hospital beds. My food shaped my world, like everyone else's does theirs, creating unique memories for each of us individually. My food was full to the brim with colour, bursting at the seams with laughter, waiting at the door in anticipation, overflowing with happiness, seasoned with a measure of sadness.

At home, we lived on rice and curries. Not just any old rice and curry, but some of the most beautifully cooked, elegantly spiced curries I have ever eaten. Always filled with Asian vegetables that had a carbon footprint as hefty as the receipts my dad came home with. Rice and curry after school every night. Rice and curry for lunch on the weekend and the same again for dinner. We didn't know any different so we never complained. We ate in congregation on the floor and we ate with our hands, all five fingers stained and scented with turmeric.

During term time, school lunches were a world away from the meals we loved at home. We used knives and forks to eat, filling up on pizza, chips, beans, burger, mashed potatoes and peas (not all at once, though sometimes I wished it could be!), followed by apple crumble, cake, tarts, biscuits and every colour of custard you can think of.

The food of my childhood was a collision of two worlds. The curry, the pink custard, the switch between hands and cutlery. British food to me was everything I ate, because I was British and therefore it followed that whatever I ate must also be British. It was only when I discovered the freedom of a driving licence and a clapped-out Renault Clio that I realized the world was bigger than my parents' kitchen and the confines of the school canteen. I discovered food magazines, supermarket aisles, takeaways (real-life food that we didn't have to cook ourselves), markets, restaurants, food stalls, Chinese supermarkets and online shopping!

Since then, I have asked myself the same question I ask even now. What is British food? Is it a fixed set of recipes? Is it the curry I grew up on? Is something British if you pour custard over it? Is it British if you eat it with cutlery? Is it really just full English breakfasts, roast beef, Yorkshire puddings, fish and chips? Type 'what is British cuisine?' into a search engine and it will tell you simply that it is 'a set of cooking traditions and practices associated with the United Kingdom'. And yet how can something so vast and varied be described in just a few vague sentences, which barely scratch the surface of its depth and complexity?

British food today is a melting pot, a bubbling mixture of cuisines that have been stirred together as people from different cultures all around the world have settled here or passed through, introducing their own colours, their own recipes, their little culinary gems, their secrets, their flavours from far and wide. Over the years, Britain has welcomed Spanish, Portuguese, Italian, Mexican, Caribbean, Chinese, Indian, Turkish, African, Arabic, Thai, Korean, Australian and North American immigrants, to list but a few, along with their ideas, influences and ingredients. This is the Britain I recognize, and the one that I set out to discover through the recipes in this book, a diverse land that I know best through the food that I have eaten and the dishes that I have come to love, and which I cook over and over again.

We never travelled much in the UK as children, but since having my own kids I have discovered nooks and crannies that I never knew existed, and so my children's 'Britain' is quite different to the one I grew up believing in. Writing this book has allowed me to travel even further, seeking out the hidden gems of the country I call my home,

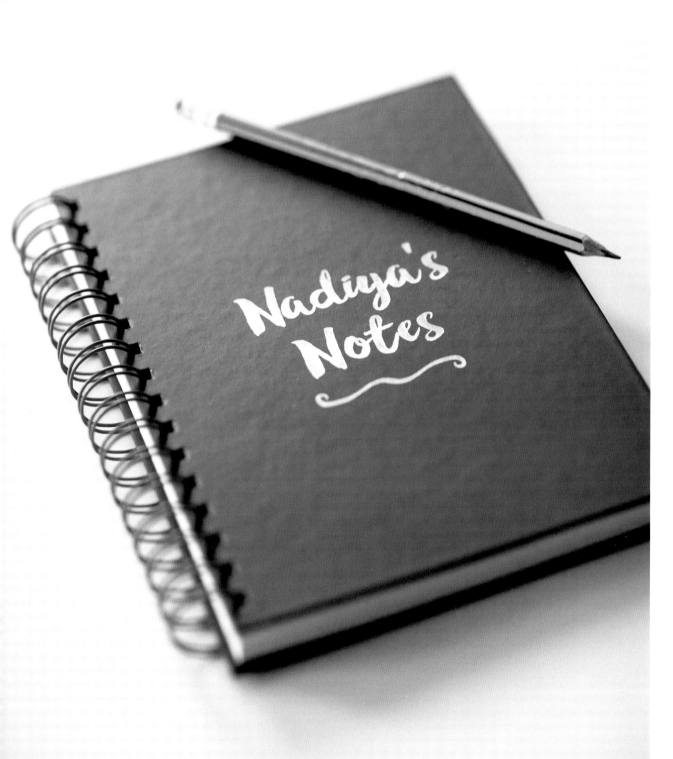

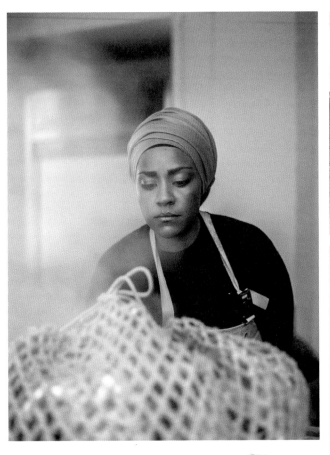

meeting exciting people who grow and farm our food, as well as innovators who have exceeded expectations, pushed boundaries and overcome adversity with their stories of imagination and hard work. These forward-thinking people are the true face of British food today, and you'll get to know some of them in my TV series, *Nadiya's British Food Adventure*. Meanwhile, the recipes I've collected together in this book will take you on a unique journey through the UK, celebrating the many culinary influences that have shaped us, and letting you taste for yourself the food and flavours that represent the real and diverse Britain that I know and love.

This book takes you through each mealtime of the day, with recipes for hearty breakfasts and brunches, speedy lunches and easy midweek meals, as well as dishes you'll love to cook when having friends over, fun ideas for parties, comforting everyday puddings and extra-special desserts. Recipes such as Masala Eggy Bread, Ploughman's Cheese & Pickle Tart, Chilli Lasagne, Minted Lamb & Apple Pasties, Fish Pie with Cinnamon Sweet Potato, Easy Chicken Tikka Masala, Fennel Welsh Cakes, Malt Tiffin, Mango & Passionfruit Jam Roly-Poly, and Eton Mess Cheesecake are just a small taster of the 120 recipes that are proudly nestled in this book and which together reflect my food journey.

My Britain is many things. It's thanks to a father – the daydreamer – who worked tirelessly to bring a bit of Bangladesh to his growing expat family. It's down to a mother – the workforce – whose greatest skill, still, is feeding us into oblivion, no matter how hard she has to work to do it. It was shaped by a brother and sister who longed to be at home, craving comfort in a bowl of solid food, because mother's food, whatever it was, meant home. It is two culinary worlds that collided spectacularly to create a grey area that is more colourful than a rainbow, with a pot of sprinkles at the end of it!

This is the Britain that I recognize and the Britain that I know so many other people will relate to. A Britain we should all be proud of, for the diversity that it offers through the food it has welcomed and the worlds it has joined together. This is not just *my* Britain, this is OUR Britain. Let's feast our eyes and appetites on the amazing food it has to offer.

Breakfast and Brunch

I often wonder who first came up with certain words to label the eating path of a day, and why each name was invented. All I can say is, thank you! I'm grateful for the breaks in our day that are dictated by the time on the clock and the rumble of our bellies. Especially the first meal of the morning. As a child, I loved breakfast – for me, it was all about the latest cereal advert on the telly, followed by a continual badgering of my dad as we walked the supermarket aisles. Not much has changed, and no matter how much I try to resist, I can still be taken in by the gimmicks of an all-singing, all-dancing, cereal-eating tiger. But breakfasts themselves have changed. They have kind of merged into elevenses, stuck their toes into brunch, walked into lunch and taken a nosedive into dinner! Some days I don't know where breakfast starts or where it ends; we can eat it pretty much all day without even realizing it. I like to think that's why we give it so many names. This chapter is a collection of my earlier-in-the-day recipes that regularly satisfy the bellies of my brood and prepare them for the day ahead.

CAYENNE EGGS BENEDICT

Serves 2

This is one of my favourite café breakfasts, for the kind of day when I've rushed out with just hot tea inside me and the intention to shamelessly shop and then ease the guilt by ordering something delicious, warm and filling. But it's also a recipe that I love to cook at home, when I have someone special over for breakfast or just want to prove to myself that I can do it as well as any café. My method simplifies the two slightly more time-consuming (some may say tricky!) elements – the poached egg and the hollandaise – helping you save time and face for when you have someone to impress (even if it's just yourself!).

1. Bring a litre of water to the boil in a small pan and leave on a medium heat.

2. Meanwhile, get a cup that is big enough to house an entire egg and a piece of cling film about 23cm square (or big enough to fit the inside of the cup). Push the cling film inside the cup.

3. Spray the inside generously with oil – this will stop the egg sticking to the cling film. Crack the egg into the cling film-covered cup. Seal it in by tying up the top and repeat with the second egg.

4. At this point, I become mesmerized by the look of a raw egg encased in cling film! Once you've finished admiring this sight, place the egg parcels in the pan of hot water for 5 minutes.

5. Have a bowl of cold water ready. When the eggs have been in the pan for 5 minutes, lift them out and immerse in the cold water.

6. Toast the muffin halves lightly until crisp around the edges. Butter them and place on your serving plates.

7. Add 1 tablespoon of olive oil to a medium pan and put on a medium heat. Add the rashers and cook them for 5 minutes, turning when required. They should be lightly crisp.

8. Put 3 rashers on each buttered muffin half.

9. Get a bowl of hot water ready. Take the eggs out of the cold water, cut off the top of the cling film and unwrap. Dunk the eggs in the hot water for 30 seconds to rewarm them. Lift out with a slotted spoon, drain on kitchen paper, then place carefully on top of the rashers.

10. Meanwhile, put the mayonnaise, milk, cayenne pepper and vinegar into a small pan. Stir on a low heat until the sauce is warm, check the seasoning, then spoon over the poached eggs. Sprinkle with chopped chives and a little more cayenne, if you like.

PREP 15 MINUTES
COOK 20 MINUTES

spray oil

2 medium eggs

1 English muffin, sliced in half horizontally

butter, for spreading

1 tablespoon olive oil

6 rashers (I use halal smoked turkey rashers, but you can use bacon)

6 tablespoons full-fat mayonnaise

1 tablespoon whole/semi-skimmed milk

½ teaspoon cayenne pepper (increase to 1 teaspoon if you like it hotter)

1 teaspoon white vinegar

1 teaspoon fresh chives, chopped

CARDAMOM BANANA DROP SCONES

Serves 4 (makes 12)

My children often begin the mornings with a sweet breakfast revolution, chanting, 'Pancakes, pancakes, pancakes,' until I drag myself out of bed. Believe me, this is no fun at 6 a.m. on a Sunday, but on the weekends the kids do tend to get their way and I often make these easy banana drop scones. (On a rushed weekday, it's rice puffs with honey. So I can see why we have revolution two days out of seven!) These are like little baby pancakes with a hidden gem inside, and are so simple to make that it's win-win for everyone. As an extra treat I make this fragrant cardamom caramel to go with them.

PREP 20 MINUTES

COOK 20 MINUTES

For the cardamom caramel

125g soft brown sugar

50g unsalted butter

125ml double cream

1½ teaspoons ground green cardamom (see tip below)

For the drop scones

140g self-raising flour

a pinch of salt

1 tablespoon caster sugar

1 large egg

150ml whole milk

1 large ripe banana, cut into 12 slices (about 1cm thick)

50g unsalted butter, for frying

1. First make the caramel. If your sugar is lumpy, rub it between your fingers to break up any big bits. Put the sugar and butter into a small pan and place on a medium heat. Cook for a few minutes, stirring all the time. As soon as the sugar has melted, take the pan off the heat.

2. Add the cream and cardamom and stir until it is all well combined. Set the caramel aside while you make the drop scones.

3. Place the flour, salt and sugar in a bowl and give it all a quick mix. Make a well in the centre and add the egg. Again, mix that in.

4. Stir in half the milk and you should get a thick paste. Add the rest of the milk and the mixture will slacken slightly, though it should still be thick. Perfect for dropping scones!

5. Put half the butter into a frying pan and place on a medium heat. Once it has melted, place the banana slices in the pan, well spaced out. Work in batches – I can fit about 6 slices in a 28cm pan.

6. Place a tablespoon of the drop scone mixture on top of each banana slice and leave to cook slowly on a medium to low heat for 4 minutes. The top layer should be covered in bubbles.

7. When the tops look less liquid and more set, turn them over with a spatula and cook for a further 3 minutes.

8. Once the drop scones are cooked, keep them warm on a plate, covered with foil, while you cook the second batch.

9. Gently reheat the caramel and serve generously alongside the warm drop scones.

Tip: If you can't find ground cardamom, crush 8 cardamom pods in a pestle and mortar or a spice grinder, discard the green pods, then grind the seeds to a fine powder.

BROWN MUSTARD POTATO RÖSTI

Serves 2

Although I often succumb to the quick fried variety when I am on the road, or when I'm just too tired to stop and make breakfast, there's nothing quite like making rösti from scratch. Even so, nobody wants to start their day having to peel, chop and boil potatoes, especially not caffeine-free at 8 a.m.! So for this recipe, my spuds keep their skins firmly on and all they need is grating, before being flavoured with delicious brown mustard seeds and served with a crisp frilly egg. You simply need a box grater and the belief that potatoes do not have to mean faff first thing in the morning.

PREP 15 MINUTES

COOK 10 MINUTES

1–2 large potatoes (approx. 300g), washed well and skins kept on

salt and black pepper, for seasoning

1 teaspoon brown mustard seeds

3 tablespoons olive oil

2 large eggs

1 tablespoon roughly torn fresh coriander

brown sauce, to serve (optional)

1. Coarsely grate the potatoes on your grater's largest setting.

2. By hand, take a small amount of the grated potato and squeeze all the excess moisture out of it. Getting rid of as much moisture as you can now will help the rösti crisp up later. Repeat with the rest of the grated potato.

3. Place the grated potato in a bowl, season with a large pinch of salt and the mustard seeds, and mix.

4. Place a medium frying pan on a medium heat (my pan is 28cm) and add 1 tablespoon of oil.

5. When the oil is hot, divide the potato mixture into two batches. Place the two mounds in the frying pan. Using the back of a spatula, flatten the mounds down and allow the potato to cook gently on a medium heat. This will take 5 minutes on one side.

6. Gently turn your rösti over and cook for another 3 minutes. They will be crisp on the outside. Transfer them carefully on to your serving plates – they may still be slightly fragile.

7. Using the same frying pan, wipe off any crumbs with kitchen paper, then add the remaining 2 tablespoons of oil and heat on a high heat until the pan is smoking.

8. Crack an egg directly into the pan – it should instantly start to frill around the edges. Once the egg has frilled, turn the heat down and allow the rest of the white to cook, making sure the yolk stays runny. This should take only a few minutes. Season the egg lightly with a pinch of salt. Repeat with the other egg (you can cook them both at once if your pan is large enough).

9. Place each frilly egg on top of a rösti, sprinkle with coriander leaves and black pepper, and serve while still warm. My kids love these with copious amounts of brown sauce, but I like the runny egg yolk to do the saucing for me.

TURMERIC TOMATOES ON AVOCADO TOAST

Serves 4

There's a lot in the news right now about the health benefits of turmeric, and this is a great way to add a bit of bright-yellow spice to the start of your day. (Better than the glass of turmeric and milk concoction that my sister is convinced tastes good! I would rather have mine with my tomatoes in the morning, as I prefer to eat my food slowly rather than the down-in-one method.) The sweetness of the tomatoes works really well with the smoky turmeric when cooked lightly over a low heat.

PREP 15 MINUTES

COOK 15 MINUTES

4 slices of sourdough (or slices of bread of your choice: white, brown, or the kind with no crusts for fussy non-crust eaters, etc.)

2 medium ripe avocados (approx. 400g)

a squeeze of lemon juice

4 tablespoons olive oil

2 cloves of garlic, finely chopped

20 ripe cherry tomatoes (approx. 400g), quartered

a good pinch of salt

½ teaspoon ground turmeric

2 tablespoons water

1. Toast the sourdough (or bread of your choice) until it's just crisp, and set aside on a serving plate.

2. Cut the avocados in half, remove the stones and scoop out the flesh. Add a squeeze of lemon juice, then mash, using the back of a fork. The lemon juice will stop the avocado going brown while you cook the tomatoes.

3. Place a frying pan on a medium heat and add the oil. Once the oil is just hot, add the crushed garlic and stir for a few seconds, keeping an eye on it to make sure it doesn't burn.

4. Add the quartered tomatoes and salt, and cook for 2 minutes.

5. Now add the turmeric and the water. Cook on a medium heat for 10 minutes, until the tomatoes have softened and broken down slightly. Be sure to keep an eye on them, making sure they don't burn. If they do start to stick, just add another tablespoon of water.

6. Spread each slice of toasted sourdough with equal amounts of the mashed avocado and top with the hot cooked tomatoes.

SMOKED PAPRIKA CORNED BEEF & BAKED BEAN WRAP

Serves 4

Although I had heard of corned beef while I was growing up, I never really came across it until about 10 years ago. Out of curiosity, I bought a tin. It then sat in my cupboard for 5 years before I even considered doing anything with it. It's certainly an acquired taste. I knew my old neighbour Norman lived on the stuff, but when I told him I was about to spice it up he was unimpressed and said it should only ever be eaten fried in slices and served with mashed potatoes and a fried egg. Of course, I did what I do best and ignored every word he said, and changed it anyway. This is my simple way of spicing up corned beef for a quick and easy meal.

1. Place a medium frying pan on a medium heat and add the oil. Once it has just warmed up, add the garlic, stir for a few seconds, then add the chopped onion. Season to taste and cook for about 5 minutes, until the onion has softened.

2. Stir in the smoked paprika and cook for 2 minutes. If the mixture begins to stick, just add a tablespoon of water and let it loosen.

3. Stir in the corned beef – it will start to break up a little.

4. Add the baked beans and cook gently for 5 minutes, making sure you keep an eye on it. The mixture is quite thick, so it will have a tendency to stick.

5. Take off the heat and stir in the chopped coriander.

6. Put the tortilla wraps into the microwave for 30 seconds, to warm them up and make them a little more flexible.

7. Place a quarter of the corned beef mixture in the centre of a warmed tortilla wrap. Fold over the two edges. Take the closest part of the wrap to you and fold over. Tuck the wrap in and roll. Cut in half at an angle.

8. Serve each wrap with a wedge of lime and a spoonful of Greek yoghurt.

PREP 15 MINUTES
COOK 15 MINUTES

1 tablespoon olive oil

1 clove of garlic, finely sliced

1 red onion (approx. 150g), chopped

salt, for seasoning

2 teaspoons smoked paprika

1 x 340g tin of corned beef, chopped into chunks

1 x 410g tin of baked beans

1 small bag of fresh coriander (30g, approx. 3 tablespoons), finely chopped

4 large tortilla wraps

1 lime, cut into 4 wedges

Greek yoghurt, to serve

GARLIC & PARSLEY EGG CUPS

Serves 6

There's a growing trend online for recipes that involve edible containers, so you can eat whatever's on the inside and enjoy the outside too. I'm talking cookie cups filled with milk, fondue served in its own edible bread bowl, and so much more. Not only does the edible exterior help things feel that bit more fun, it also makes you look so much more accomplished in the kitchen! And let's not forget – if the casing is edible, think of all the washing-up you don't have to do. So I've joined the trend, and used delicious garlic bread as a carrier for some beautifully cooked eggs.

PREP 15 MINUTES

COOK 20–35 MINUTES

12 slices of white bread

80g garlic butter

12 small–medium eggs

12 pinches of salt

12 sprigs of fresh curly parsley

1. Preheat the oven to 180°C/160°C fan/gas 4.

2. Cut all 4 crusts off the bread (don't be alarmed – don't throw them away, put them on a baking tray ready to dry out in the oven, then blitz and make into breadcrumbs).

3. Using a rolling pin, roll each slice of bread until it is completely flat. This makes it much easier to work with later and gives you a crispier cup.

4. Melt the garlic butter (if you don't have any at home, just take unsalted butter and add a minced clove of garlic to it).

5. Brush the inside of a 12-hole muffin tray with some of the melted garlic butter.

6. Line the inside of each hole with a slice of flattened bread, making sure to push the bread right into the base and edges. Don't worry about being exact, as they are not meant to look identical.

7. Brush the inside of the bread with the remainder of the melted garlic butter.

8. Drop an egg into each cavity, then season them all with a pinch of salt and top with a parsley sprig.

9. Bake on the middle shelf of the oven for 18–20 minutes if you like a runny yolk. If, however, you prefer a firm yolk, leave to bake in the oven for 35 minutes.

Tip: Be sure to get small to medium eggs or there could be a serious case of egg spillage.

CINNAMON & PINEAPPLE FRENCH TOAST

Serves 2

I'm all for dishing out credit where credit is due. I once heard a conversation between my husband and his sister about how, as children, they used to eat French toast with pineapple. My initial reaction was 'oooooh' – it sounded sophisticated and unusual . . . until it turned out to be a ring of tinned pineapple in the centre, not fresh as I'd imagined. But when I took my mother-in-law's humble tinned pineapple idea and tried it for myself, I discovered that sometimes things are best left simple. So here's her recipe, which I've not changed too much, except for the addition of cinnamon just to lift it.

PREP 15 MINUTES
COOK 10 MINUTES

1 x 435g tin of
crushed pineapple
(278g drained weight)

2 tablespoons soft
brown sugar

½ teaspoon ground cinnamon

2 medium eggs

100ml whole milk

1 tablespoon caster sugar

4 slices of white bread

30g unsalted butter

2 tablespoons Greek yoghurt

a drizzle of honey

1. Drain the tinned pineapple in a colander, then take small handfuls of it and make sure you squeeze out all the excess moisture. Nothing worse than moisture and bread – bad combination! Put the pineapple into a bowl with the sugar and cinnamon, stir and set aside.

2. Using a large plate with sides, crack in the eggs and add the milk and sugar. Whisk lightly with a fork.

3. Take the 4 slices of bread and sandwich them together in pairs with half the pineapple mixture.

4. Put a frying pan on a medium heat, add half the butter and leave it to melt.

5. Once the butter has melted, dip the first pineapple sandwich into the egg mixture, turning it over so it is coated on both sides. Place in the pan with the melted butter. (Alternatively, if you have a pan big enough to cook both sandwiches at the same time, add all the butter to the pan at once and cook them together.)

6. Cook on a medium heat for 2 minutes, until the bread is a golden colour and the eggy bits have cooked through.

7. Now turn over gently, using a spatula and a fork (for extra insurance), and cook on the other side for 2 minutes. Place on a piece of kitchen paper to drain off any excess butter.

8. Now do the same with the other pineapple sandwich. Add the remaining butter, dip both sides, fry both sides and drain.

9. Cut the sandwiches in half, and serve with a tablespoon of yoghurt drizzled with a little honey.

BLACK PEPPER &
SMOKED SALMON OMELETTE

Serves 2

Whether it's a plain and simple dinner for one, or something for feeding a crowd, an omelette is quick, versatile and can be flavoured and changed around in so many ways. The mixture of smoked salmon and black pepper in this one makes a winning combination. So often, black pepper is used as seasoning and you can't really taste the pepper itself, but if you treat it like a spice, rather than a seasoning, that's when it really comes into its own.

1. Crack the eggs into a bowl and season with the salt and pepper.

2. Place a medium frying pan (about 20cm, preferably non-stick) on a high heat and add half the butter. Once the butter has melted, pour in half the egg mixture.

3. Gently stir the egg mixture three or four times, scraping away at the edges. Lower the heat to medium.

4. Add the slices of salmon all over the top, then the chives. Lower the heat completely, cover and cook for 3 minutes.

5. Remove the omelette and keep warm on a plate, covered with foil. Put the pan back on the hob, turn the heat up to medium, add the remaining butter and cook the second omelette in the same way as before.

6. I like to eat this just as is, but if you are feeling hungrier it also tastes pretty good sandwiched between slices of buttered wholemeal bread.

Photos overleaf →

PREP 15 MINUTES
COOK 10 MINUTES

6 medium eggs

½ teaspoon salt

2 teaspoons freshly ground black pepper

50g unsalted butter

100g smoked salmon, sliced

2 tablespoons chopped fresh chives

buttered wholemeal bread, to serve (optional)

CHERRY, ALMOND & NUTMEG TARTS

Serves 8

Pop Tarts: we've surely all heard of them, and I imagine most people have probably tried one too. Or do I only speak for myself when I say that Pop Tart curiosity once got the better of me and as a teenager I felt I just had to taste this American breakfast phenomenon? It was quite something watching it pop out of the toaster like the biscuit equivalent of a 5-year-old on sugar. But it became an entirely different tale when my eagerness led to a very burnt mouth. This recipe is my more grown-up interpretation. The tarts are sweet, easy to make and have a hint of spice. But like my encounter with their 1999 counterpart, these too can scald an unsuspecting mouth if served hot. So please eat with caution.

1. Dust the surface of the worktop with plenty of icing sugar and roll out the pastry to a 30 x 35cm rectangle. Place it on a piece of baking paper and then on a tray. (This will help you move the pastry in and out of the fridge.)

2. Cut right down the middle of the pastry lengthways, giving you two long equal rectangles. Now make three cuts across widthways to give you eight equal rectangles. Place in the fridge.

3. Put the jam in a bowl, add the ground nutmeg and mix.

4. Have a baking tray lined with baking paper ready. To each rectangle of pastry, add 1 teaspoon of jam on one side, making sure to avoid the edges. (Don't be tempted to add extra jam – I once learned this the hard way!)

5. Brush the edges with the eggwash and fold over the other half of the pastry. With the tip of a dinner knife, press down to seal the edges. This is crucial unless you enjoy flowing molten lava jam.

6. Do the same with the remaining seven pastries. Brush the tops with the eggwash and place in the fridge for 20 minutes.

7. Preheat the oven to 200°C/180°C fan/gas 6.

8. Take the pastries out of the fridge and bake on the middle shelf of the oven for 20–25 minutes. Place on a wire rack to cool.

9. To make the icing, put the icing sugar, water and almond extract into a bowl and mix to a smooth paste. Cover the tops of the pastries with icing and sprinkle with crushed toasted almonds.

Tip: If you want to eat these warm, I don't recommend using the toaster, but you can quickly zap them in the microwave.

PREP 30 MINUTES,
PLUS CHILLING
COOK 20 MINUTES

For the tarts

icing sugar (approx. 20g), for dusting

500g shortcrust pastry

150g cherry jam

½ teaspoon ground nutmeg

1 medium egg, beaten lightly

For the almond icing

100g icing sugar, sifted

1½ tablespoons water

¼ teaspoon almond extract

20g toasted flaked almonds

MASALA EGGY BREAD

Serves 4

Hands up who loves eggy bread? Well, everyone in my house loves it in every form and we are always looking for new ways of eating the stuff. Which is why I couldn't resist including two recipes for it, one savoury and one sweet (see also Cinnamon & Pineapple French Toast, page 24). It really is a good base to take on all sorts of flavours, and this eggy bread recipe uses up some of the ingredients that I always have at home. Rather than putting the extra ingredients into the egg mixture at the start, here they are added carefully afterwards, to keep all the flavour on top of the toast. You will need a spatula and a steady hand.

PREP 15 MINUTES
COOK 10 MINUTES

1 red onion (approx. 150g), chopped

1 teaspoon whole cumin seeds

½ teaspoon chilli flakes

1 tablespoon chopped fresh coriander

½ teaspoon salt

4 medium eggs

4 slices of bread

50g butter

1. Put the chopped onion, cumin seeds, chilli flakes, coriander and salt into a bowl. Using your hands, squeeze all the ingredients to macerate and soften them. Set aside.

2. Crack the eggs on to a rimmed plate or shallow dish and season. Whisk lightly, using a fork.

3. Take a slice of bread and dip it in the egg mixture. Do the same with the other pieces of bread and set aside on another plate.

4. Place a large frying pan on a medium heat, then add half the butter and allow it to melt gently.

5. Add 2 slices of soaked bread to the pan and top each with a quarter of the onion mix. Cook for 2 minutes.

6. Using a wide spatula, gently and quickly flip the bread slices over. The onion side, facing down, should now cook for a further 2 minutes. Put the slices on a plate and cover with foil to keep them warm.

7. Wipe out the pan with kitchen paper, add the rest of the butter and fry the other 2 slices of bread the same way.

TOASTED TEACAKES WITH CINNAMON DATE BUTTER

—— Makes 6 teacakes and 300g of date butter ——

When my youngest child was born I suddenly had three kids under the age of four! While my older two went to nursery for the afternoon, I would sometimes tear myself away from the housework, and treat myself to fruit toast and an Earl Grey tea. I love the tart, sticky fruit in a warm toasted teacake. But while my daughter could easily eat her way through six tiny boxes of raisins in a walk to the park, if they were baked into something she simply would not touch them, picking them out and flinging them aside. So I created this recipe for her, and for anyone who doesn't like raisins. The teacakes are served with a delicious homemade butter that's sweetened with sticky dates. There's nothing better.

**PREP 1 HOUR 10 MINUTES,
PLUS PROVING
COOK 20 MINUTES**

For the teacakes

150ml whole milk

50g unsalted butter, room temperature

1 medium egg

375g strong bread flour

½ teaspoon salt

7g fast-action yeast

1 teaspoon ground cinnamon

zest of 1 orange

50g golden caster sugar

2 teaspoons vegetable oil, for greasing

For the cinnamon and date butter

160g dried dates

150ml boiling water

600ml double cream

½ teaspoon rock salt

½ teaspoon ground cinnamon

1. For the teacakes, place the milk and butter in a jug or small bowl and microwave until the butter has melted – or you can do this in a small pan. Don't boil the milk, just warm it enough for the butter to melt. Then whisk in the egg and set aside.

2. Place the flour in the bowl of a stand mixer, then add the salt to one side of the bowl, yeast on the other side, and the cinnamon, orange zest and caster sugar. Give it all a mix and make a well in the centre. Pour in the milk mixture and give it all a good stir to just combine.

3. Attach the dough hook to the mixer and knead on medium speed for 5 minutes, until the dough is smooth and elastic. If you are doing it by hand, knead the dough on a lightly oiled surface for 10 minutes.

4. Put the dough back into the bowl, then cover with cling film and leave in a warm place for at least an hour, until the dough has doubled in size. This will depend on how warm the room is, so don't fret if it takes longer than an hour.

5. Grease two baking trays lightly with a little oil.

6. Once proved, take the dough and knock out the air by pushing it down with your knuckles. Roll it out into a sausage shape and cut it into six equal pieces. Roll each one into a ball, then, using a spoon, flatten them so they are about 1cm thick and place on the baking trays. Take two pieces of cling film and lightly oil them. Cover the dough with the cling film, oil side down and leave to prove again for 1 hour in a warm place.

Recipe continues overleaf →

7. Meanwhile, start the cinnamon and date butter. Put the dates into a bowl, pour over the hot water and set aside for 20 minutes.

8. Put the cream into the bowl of a stand mixer and begin whisking. Now this is the fun bit. No need to worry about over-whipping, because this is exactly what you want to do. From start to finish, the process will take 5 minutes with the mixer on high. As soon as the cream has gone from soft peaks, to stiff peaks, to over-whipped, the cream will start to gather and look almost crumbly. You will know it is ready when you can see water in the base of the bowl. Now you have butter.

9. Place a sieve over a bowl and pour the mixture in. Leave the water to drip through the sieve. You can help the process along by pressing the butter against the sieve using the back of a spoon.

10. Once the teacake dough has proved, preheat the oven to 190°C/170°C fan/gas 5. Take off the cling film and bake the teacakes for 15–20 minutes. Then take them out of the oven and leave to cool on a wire rack.

11. Transfer the soft drained butter into a bowl.

12. Drain the dates and squeeze out the water. Blitz the dates roughly and add to the butter with the salt and cinnamon. Mix well, then cover and chill in the fridge until needed.

13. To serve, slice the teacakes in half, toast them and spread with the date butter.

PEANUT GRANOLA

Makes 820g

We love granola in our house, usually served on honey yoghurt with bananas sliced on top, the ripest ones we can find. I know granola is easy enough to buy, but it's also just as easy to make, rather like making flapjacks but without the cooling and slicing bit. My family all love peanuts too, so this is our favourite granola, mixed with all sorts of other delights including linseeds and a cheeky addition of dark chocolate chips.

PREP 20 MINUTES
COOK 45 MINUTES

100g unsalted butter

60g runny honey

100g dark brown muscovado sugar

200g porridge oats

100g golden linseeds

50g sunflower seeds

50g salted peanuts

100g dried figs, roughly chopped

100g dark chocolate chips (or milk, white, butterscotch or even peanut butter chips, if you can get them)

1. Preheat the oven to 180°C/160°C fan/gas 4.

2. Place the butter, honey, and muscovado sugar in a small pan and warm on a medium heat till the butter has dissolved and the sugar has melted. Take off the heat.

3. Put the oats, linseeds, sunflower seeds, peanuts and figs into a large bowl and mix to combine. Add the melted butter mixture and stir again so that all the nuts and oats are coated. Place on a large baking tray and spread out.

4. Bake in the oven for 40–45 minutes, making sure to give the mixture a stir every 15 minutes. If you find it getting dark sooner, take the mixture out.

5. Leave to cool on the tray. Once the mixture is completely cool, mix in the chips.

6. Transfer to an airtight container, and eat with yoghurt and sliced bananas, like we do, or however you prefer.

For the Love of Lunch

I'm not always sure how I feel about lunch. It's that moment right in the middle of the day when we're often too busy to stop what we're doing, and then the instant it's over we're already far too busy thinking about what we fancy for dinner. It's like the middle child of the food world, doesn't quite know where it belongs. But what I do know is that it's a vital part of the day and actually very important. For all those middle children out there (don't worry, I'm one too), it's time we realized you are worth stopping for, you are worth some embellishment, and you are there to help us remember why it's good to pause and take a breath. Here is a collection of simple lunch recipes that are easy, satisfying and – most of all – worth stopping for.

SESAME CHICKEN WITH QUICK KIMCHI

Serves 4

This recipe combines two of my favourite things: the first is delicious sesame chicken (like they sell at my local Chinese takeaway) and the second is kimchi, which is definitely the 'in' thing right now. People have eaten kimchi for centuries, but it's finally made it on to the menu at my local lunch stop-off and at last it's getting the recognition it deserves. I love its bold flavour, which pairs well with the subtlety of the chicken. Even better, this is my quick version of kimchi, with no fermenting required!

1. Put all the sesame seeds on a plate and mix together.

2. Crack the egg on to another rimmed plate and beat lightly.

3. Season the chicken breasts lightly and dip in the egg. Then dip into the sesame seeds. Set the chicken aside on a separate plate.

4. Heat the oil in a large frying pan and fry the butterflied chicken on a medium to low heat for 5 minutes on either side. If your pan isn't large enough to fit all four pieces at once, just add half the oil at a time and fry them in two batches. Bear in mind that the chicken is coated in seeds that are prone to burning quickly, so be careful and keep a close eye on them.

5. In the meantime, prepare the salad by putting the salt, spring onions, brown sugar, garlic, ginger, fish sauce and chilli into a bowl. Use your hands to macerate the mixture.

6. Now add the cabbage and, again using your hands, squeeze that cabbage together with everything else in the bowl. This will give it the fermented look of kimchi without the actual fermentation process.

7. Drain the chicken on kitchen paper, then cut into thin slices. Serve piles of the kimchi salad topped with slices of sesame chicken.

PREP 25 MINUTES
COOK 12 MINUTES

For the sesame chicken

100g sesame seeds

25g black sesame seeds

1 large egg, beaten

4 chicken breasts, butterflied (see page 109)

salt, for seasoning

5 tablespoons olive oil

For the kimchi salad

½ teaspoon salt

2 spring onions, thinly sliced

1 teaspoon soft brown sugar

2 cloves of garlic, grated

20g fresh ginger, peeled and grated

1 tablespoon fish sauce

1 large chilli, thinly sliced (seeds removed if you prefer less heat)

150g each of red cabbage and white cabbage (about ¼ of a head for each), thinly sliced, on a mandolin if you have one

PLOUGHMAN'S CHEESE & PICKLE TART

Serves 8

People say not to go food shopping when hungry, but I disagree, and a ploughman's sandwich is my favourite thing to eat while I do the weekly shop. That combination of strong cheese and tart chunky pickle is my inspiration for this recipe. Cut through the cheesy filling and you'll find a hidden layer of pickle waiting to tantalize your taste buds, with a hint of heat from the pastry.

**PREP 25 MINUTES,
PLUS CHILLING
COOK 1 HOUR 10 MINUTES**

350g shortcrust pastry

1 teaspoon paprika

plain flour, for dusting

4 medium eggs

150ml whole milk

200g sandwich pickle
(small chunks)

250g mature Cheddar
cheese, grated

1. Take the block of shortcrust pastry, flatten it out slightly and sprinkle all over with the paprika. Fold the edges in over the top, then knead the pastry until all the paprika is incorporated. If the pastry starts to stick to the worktop, dust with flour.

2. Wrap the pastry in cling film and place in the fridge for 15 minutes. Meanwhile, preheat the oven to 180°C/160°C fan/gas 4 and put a baking tray in to heat up.

3. Dust the work surface with flour and roll out the pastry to the thickness of a pound coin and large enough to cover the base and sides of a 23cm diameter, 3–4cm deep, loose-bottomed flan tin.

4. Line the inside of the tin with the rolled-out pastry. Press it into the edges, right into the grooves, leaving some overhang. Pierce the base all over with a fork. This stops it puffing up while baking.

5. Cover the base and sides with a large piece of baking paper and fill with baking beans to weigh the pastry down. Take the hot baking tray out of the oven and place the prepared tart tin on it.

6. Bake for 25 minutes, then take out of the oven, remove the paper and baking beans, and bake for another 15 minutes.

7. Meanwhile, put your eggs into a jug and lightly whisk. Add the milk and stir.

8. Once the tart shell is out of the oven, spread the pickle all over the base and cover evenly with the grated cheese.

9. Pour in the milky egg mixture and place the whole tray back in the oven, on the middle shelf, for 25–30 minutes, until the filling is set and golden with just a very slight wobble in the middle.

10. Once the tart is cool enough to handle, slice off the pastry overhang using a sharp serrated knife. Leave to cool in the tin for 30 minutes, then transfer to a wire rack to cool completely.

Tip: This tart is best served lukewarm or cold and is great for picnics, lunchboxes or food on the go. It can also be frozen for up to a month – defrost it in the fridge before eating.

CARAWAY SALMON WITH
RED PEPPER & QUINOA SALAD

Serves 4

I'm not a massive fan of cold salads. I eat them because somewhere in my subconscious mind doing so makes me feel better about myself. But if I can help it, I prefer a salad that has some sort of warm element to it. I like warmth in all its forms, and will whack the central heating on 30 minutes before a bath, just on the off-chance that I might feel cold when I get out. My father has even threatened to surgically implant a halogen heater under my skin to stop me complaining about the cold. That's why I like this salad: it's a vibrant and fragrant combination of quinoa and caraway, topped with a warm piece of crispy-skinned salmon.

1. Put the quinoa into a small pan and add the water. Bring to the boil on a high heat, then turn down to medium and simmer until all the water has evaporated – this should take about 20 minutes. Once the water has gone, leave on the lowest heat for a couple of minutes to dry the quinoa, stirring frequently to make sure it isn't sticking to the bottom of the pan. If your packet of quinoa comes with different instructions, you can follow those instead.

2. Meanwhile, put a frying pan on a medium heat and add 4 table-spoons of oil. When the oil is warm, add the caraway seeds, and once you hear the seeds popping add the onion and red pepper. Season immediately with the salt and cook for 10 minutes, until it has all softened.

3. Add the zest and juice of the lemon, then add the quinoa and parsley and mix it all through.

4. Divide the quinoa mixture between four plates and put some watercress on top.

5. Clean the frying pan with kitchen paper. Place on a high heat.

6. Drizzle the salmon fillets with the rest of the oil and massage all over, then season and place in the hot pan, skin side down. Lower the heat to medium and cook for 4–8 minutes, until the skin is crisp and the salmon has turned opaque most of the way up (how long this takes will depend on the thickness of your salmon).

7. Turn the fillets over and cook for a further minute on the other side. Place on the plates next to the quinoa and watercress.

8. That's both the hot and cold elements, but I think the halogen heater idea could still catch on.

PREP 20 MINUTES
COOK 30 MINUTES

160g quinoa

480ml water

7 tablespoons olive oil

2 teaspoons caraway seeds

1 small white onion
(approx. 150g), thinly sliced

1 large red pepper (approx.
150g), thinly sliced

½ teaspoon salt, plus more
for seasoning

zest and juice of ½ a lemon

a small handful of fresh curly
parsley, chopped

4 small handfuls of watercress

4 skin-on salmon fillets
(approx. 115g each)

CREAMY BROCCOLI & OREGANO PASTA

Serves 4

Mmmmmm, creamy pasta. Not like the stuff from a packet that was dished up for school dinners or the stuff that comes out of a tin. The real deal. Quick, easy and delicious, three of my favourite traits where cooking is involved. When this first appeared on their plates, everyone else in my household was not so sure. But I wasn't having any of it. 'The kitchen is not a restaurant,' I said. 'You will eat what you are given.' That was to the 10-year-old, the 9-year-old, the 6-year-old AND the 35-year-old! I still thought they would take some convincing but – who knew! – hand your family a plate of cream and garlic, mix in some oregano and pasta, and suddenly they stop complaining!

PREP 15 MINUTES

COOK 15 MINUTES

a large pinch of salt

300g dried spaghetti

200g broccoli florets, cut into bite-size pieces

400ml double cream

7 cloves of garlic, kept whole but crushed lightly under a knife

1½ teaspoons dried oregano

100g Parmesan cheese, finely grated

zest of 1 lemon

1. Put a large pan of salted water on to boil. Once it's boiling, add the pasta and cook according to the instructions on the packet. Or if you're a dab hand at pasta boiling, cook the pasta to your personal taste. During the last 2 minutes of cooking, add the broccoli.

2. Meanwhile, pour the cream into a small pan, add the garlic cloves and place on a medium heat. Cook the cream for 4–5 minutes, until it has reduced by just under half and has thickened.

3. Use a fork to find the garlic cloves in the pan and crush them with the back of the fork against the side of the pan. Add the oregano and Parmesan, stir and keep warm.

4. Drain the spaghetti and broccoli, keeping the cooking water.

5. Add the spaghetti and broccoli to the thickened cream mixture, season and stir. If the mixture is a little dry, add a splash of the cooking water.

6. Grate some lemon zest on top of each plate as you serve it. This will cut through the creaminess. I like to just grate it on top at the end, so it doesn't mix in and get lost among everything else.

TAMARIND PRAWN COCKTAIL SANDWICH

Serves 4

Retro as they are, I love a good prawn cocktail. And what's even better in my opinion is a prawn cocktail between two slices of bread. In case you're wondering where I tasted my first-ever prawn cocktail, the answer to your question is my dad's Indian restaurant. (Yes, that's right! My dad served prawn cocktail in his Indian restaurant!) I don't know if it was authentic or anywhere near the real thing – all I remember is that it was delicious, rich, creamy and full of prawns. This is my take on the classic, but in sandwich form and with my own little twists.

1. Put the cooked prawns into a bowl, making sure not to tip in any excess moisture.

2. Now take the seafood sticks and start peeling them in strips lengthways, until all the flesh is shredded, or slice thinly with a knife if yours are difficult to peel. Add them to the prawns.

3. Put the mayonnaise, tamarind paste and pink peppercorns into a separate bowl. Give this all a thorough mix and add to the seafood. Stir it all together.

4. Butter your bread slices. (I like to put lashings on. My rule is if I can't see my teeth marks in the butter, there's no point in eating it!)

5. Lay some shredded lettuce on top of half the buttered bread slices and spoon on the prawn cocktail mixture.

6. Put the rest of the buttered bread slices on top. Now, if like my dad you want to serve this on a bed of lettuce in a tall martini glass, by all means do so. There are no rules.

PREP 15 MINUTES
NO COOK

220g peeled and cooked king prawns

80g seafood sticks (5 sticks)

60g full-fat mayonnaise

1 tablespoon tamarind paste

1 teaspoon pink peppercorns, crushed

8 slices of white bread

butter, for spreading

8 leaves of little gem lettuce, shredded (we've all been there, when you go in to bite a sandwich and manage to take the entire leaf of lettuce with you upon exit, so let's avoid that)

CORIANDER-CRUSTED CHICKEN LIVER SALAD

Serves 4

I can picture the dread on people's faces when they see the words 'liver' or 'onion' or – heaven forbid! – 'liver and onion'! I grew up eating liver curry as if it was what all children went home and ate. But saying that, I once came home from school to be greeted by a 4-foot defrosting river fish in the bathtub, so what was normal to me was perhaps unusual for many! My mum makes a mean liver curry, but I think that adding a sauce just masks the flavour of the livers, which I quite enjoy eating pink, much to my mother's disgust. So what I like to do is cook them lightly enough that they don't lose their flavour but so they also take on some of the spices they are coated in. Here they're served with delicious, warm, cooked onions. Let's make livers more than just tolerable – let's celebrate them!

PREP 20 MINUTES
COOK 10 MINUTES

35g plain flour

½ teaspoon salt, plus more for seasoning

4 teaspoons ground coriander

5 tablespoons olive oil

500g chicken livers, cleaned and prepared

2 red onions (approx. 300g), thinly sliced

2 tablespoons water

1 teaspoon chilli flakes

4 large handfuls of green salad leaves

1. Put the flour, salt and coriander on a plate and mix together so the spice is distributed.

2. Have another plate handy while you dip each piece of liver into the spiced flour mix. Once dipped, set aside on the second plate. This light coating will give the livers an aromatic crust when fried.

3. Put a frying pan on a medium heat and add 3 tablespoons of oil. Once the oil is warm, add the chicken liver pieces and fry for 3 minutes. Turn each piece over and fry for another 3 minutes.

4. Take the livers out of the pan and place on a plate lined with kitchen paper to soak up any excess oil.

5. Add the remaining 2 tablespoons of oil to the same pan (don't wipe it out, as you want all the flavour from the livers) and add the sliced red onions. Because of the flour left in the pan the onions may begin to stick, so add the water – this will evaporate, but it will stop the onions sticking.

6. Cook the onions for about 2 minutes. They will begin to wilt and soften slightly. Now season and add the chilli flakes. Cook for another minute.

7. Meanwhile, put a large handful of green salad on each plate.

8. Put the livers back into the pan of onions and stir through to warm for about 20 seconds.

9. Top each plate of green salad with the liver and onion! There – we said the two words together and it didn't even hurt, and neither will this dish.

CORONATION TURKEY JACKET POTATO

Serves 4

I had a friend at high school called Elizabeth who used to eat a Coronation chicken baguette for lunch every single day. There we'd all sit, at our usual table, scoffing enormous cheesy pizzas, chips and beans, and chocolate cake with pink custard for afters, while she tucked into her baguette yet again! It was the same for 5 years until the day we left school. I always wondered what was so special about that sandwich. I was tempted to ask for a bite in exchange for a soggy, vinegar-soaked chip, but it seemed too important to her. My curiosity stayed with me, even after that school and its awful bottle-green uniform were left behind, and it inspired me to create my own version, but with a jacket potato. It's become a firm family favourite.

PREP 15 MINUTES
COOK 25 MINUTES

4 potatoes
(approx. 200g each)

1 tablespoon olive oil

400g turkey breast, diced

a pinch of salt

3 tablespoons mayonnaise

2 tablespoons Greek yoghurt

1 teaspoon curry powder

1 tablespoon sweet
mango chutney

3 spring onions, thinly sliced

green salad, to serve

1. Put a piece of kitchen paper on a microwaveable dish and place your potatoes on top.

2. Microwave the potatoes on a high heat for 22 minutes. If they are still not done, keep cooking them in 2-minute intervals, checking after each blast.

3. Meanwhile, place a frying pan on a medium heat and add the oil. When it's warm, add the turkey and a pinch of salt and gently cook, making sure to stir every few minutes. It should take 6–8 minutes to cook.

4. Once the turkey is cooked, set aside and allow it to cool. If we were to put the mayonnaise mixture in with the hot turkey, the mixture might split and become runny. So to avoid disaster we have to exercise a tiny bit of patience. Something I don't have! That's why I know it will split.

5. Put the mayonnaise, yoghurt, curry powder, mango chutney and two-thirds of the spring onions into a separate bowl and give it all a thorough mix.

6. Once the turkey has cooled and is just slightly warm, not scorching hot, add to the mayo mix and stir through.

7. Split the potatoes in half and add the Coronation turkey. Sprinkle with the remaining spring onions.

8. This is perfect for that post-Christmas period, when there is way too much turkey left over and you are fed up with turkey sandwiches. I like to serve it with a simple green salad, and there is no need for any salad dressing when you have this lovely Coronation sauce on your plate.

FENNEL, CAULIFLOWER
& CHEESE FRITTATA

Serves 2

Although there is something quite heart-warming and special about a classic cauliflower cheese, I love nothing better than tampering with recipes, and since being introduced to the dish by a friend, I have tried so many different variations of it. My friend grew up in a traditional English home, a world away from the home I was brought up in, but we love nothing more than to share, exchange and fuse our recipes. The simple addition of fennel really elevates the flavour of the cauliflower and makes this already so versatile vegetable even more delicious.

1. Place a 20cm frying pan on a medium to low heat. Add the fennel seeds and toast them lightly, moving them around every now and again. Make sure they don't burn. You will know the seeds are ready when they begin to pop. This will only take a few minutes.

2. Once the seeds are toasted, place them in a pestle and mortar and grind them down.

3. Heat the grill to high. Put the pan back on the heat and add the oil. When it has heated up, add the spring onions and cauliflower and cook for 3 minutes, until the cauliflower has softened.

4. Now add the salt and the ground fennel seeds, and cook for a further minute.

5. Meanwhile crack the eggs into a bowl and lightly whisk. Add three-quarters of the cheese to the egg and set the remainder aside.

6. Add the egg/cheese mix to the pan and turn the heat up to high. Give it all a good mix, making sure the cauliflower is distributed. Turn the heat down to low to medium, cover and cook for 3–4 minutes, until almost set on top.

7. Take off the lid. Sprinkle with the extra cheese and place under a very hot grill for 1 minute, until the frittata is set on top and the cheese is golden and bubbling.

8. You could use this as a replacement for cauliflower and cheese in your main meal, if you wanted. Give it a try.

PREP 15 MINUTES
COOK 15 MINUTES

1 teaspoon fennel seeds

2 tablespoons olive oil

2–3 spring onions
(approx. 30g), thinly sliced

150g cauliflower
(about ½ a medium head),
thinly sliced

¼ teaspoon salt

4 large eggs

25g Red Leicester cheese,
grated

25g mature Cheddar cheese,
grated

GINGER TUNA NOODLE SOUP

Serves 2

When we were poorly as children, and even as teenagers, my dad would make the creamiest mash and top it with some tomato soup. This is my children's equivalent. When they are not feeling well, this is what they like to eat. It's a combination of various things they love, all nestled in a warming, tangy broth and topped with seared tuna. They like it so much that they want it whether they are sick or not.

PREP 20 MINUTES
COOK 10 MINUTES

2 tablespoons olive oil

a pinch of salt and pepper, for seasoning

2 tuna steaks
(approx. 150g each)

750ml vegetable stock

2 rice noodle nests
(approx. 60g each)

20g fresh ginger, peeled and sliced into thin matchsticks

2 small green chillies, thinly sliced (seeds taken out if you don't want it too spicy)

6 leaves of fresh mint, thinly sliced

2 spring onions, thinly sliced

½ a lime, cut into 2 wedges (optional)

1. The key to a dish like this is chopping and prepping everything beforehand. Then it's just a case of putting it all together.

2. Put a small frying pan on a medium heat and add the oil. Season the tuna steaks on both sides, place them in the pan and cook on a medium to low heat for 2 minutes on either side. Your fish should be brown on the outside but with a pink centre.

3. Take the tuna steaks out of the pan, put on a plate and wrap with foil to keep warm.

4. Bring the vegetable stock to the boil in a large pan, then add the 2 nests of noodles. Bring back to the boil, then lower the heat and allow the noodles to simmer for 4 minutes.

5. Place the ginger, chillies, mint and spring onions in a bowl and mix together.

6. Divide the noodles between two deep bowls and pour the broth on top.

7. Slice the tuna steaks into strips and place on to the noodles, then top with the prepared mixed garnishes.

8. Serve each bowl with a lime wedge, if you like.

FISH CURRY WITH WATERCRESS & LEMON COUSCOUS

— Serves 4 —

Available all year round at the supermarket, often mixed with other leafy greens as part of a salad, watercress really comes into its own when cooked. It has a sweet peppery flavour and cooks down much like spinach, but with more kick. An ideal fish for this curry is tilapia, a freshwater fish that is cheap and easy to prepare, with a mild taste that works well with the peppery watercress. Or you can use any other filleted non-smoked fish, like cod or haddock.

PREP 20 MINUTES
COOK 40 MINUTES

For the lemon couscous
240g couscous

1 tablespoon butter

1 lemon

½ teaspoon salt

a large handful of pea shoots or microherbs, to garnish

For the curry
700g skinless tilapia or white fish fillets, defrosted if frozen, cut into chunks

1 teaspoon paprika

1 teaspoon ground turmeric

1 teaspoon salt

3 tablespoons olive oil

3 cloves of garlic, crushed

1 small onion, finely chopped

1 small green chilli, finely chopped

½ teaspoon ground cumin

1 teaspoon ground coriander

200ml water

85g watercress, finely chopped

1. Put the couscous into a medium to large bowl (one that has room for the couscous to grow). Add boiling water until the top of the couscous is covered with 1cm of water. Add the butter, then cover with cling film and leave for 20 minutes.

2. To make the curry, put the fish into a bowl, and sprinkle in the paprika and ½ teaspoon of turmeric. Mix well, making sure to get all the fish covered with the spices. Sprinkle over a pinch of salt.

3. Place a large non-stick frying pan on a medium heat and add the oil. Add the fish to the pan and cook over a high heat for 3–4 minutes on each side, until the fish is cooked all the way through and has a golden crust all over. Take it out of the pan and leave to one side.

4. Add the garlic, onions, chilli (deseeded if you want less heat) and ½ teaspoon of salt to the same pan and cook for 5 minutes on a low to medium heat, until the onions have softened. Add ½ teaspoon of turmeric, the cumin and coriander and cook for a few minutes. The spices will be dry, so add the water at this point and leave to cook gently on a low heat for a couple more minutes.

5. Add the watercress, then cover the pan and cook for 2 minutes, until it has wilted.

6. Return the fish and any resting juices to the pan and mix through gently, just enough to warm the fish.

7. Meanwhile, take the cling film off the couscous and fluff up with a fork. Zest the lemon and add to the bowl along with the salt. Cut the rest of the lemon into wedges.

8. Serve the curry with the couscous on the side, garnished with pea shoots or microherbs and the lemon wedges.

CHILLI LASAGNE

Serves 6–8

In my 10 years of being a mother I have found so many way of eating chilli: on a potato, on a bus, in a wrap, during a swimming lesson, on chips with the neighbours . . . I have a feeling lots of people will relate to this! Chilli is versatile, quick, easy and requires very little clear-up. So this is my version of a Mexican chilli, but instead of wrapping it in tortillas I am using the tortillas like lasagne sheets. I have also adapted my version so it's suitable for vegetarians.

1. Preheat the oven to 220°C/200°C fan/gas 7. Have a 28 x 23cm baking dish ready.

2. Put the oil into a large non-stick pan and set on a medium heat. Add the garlic, onion, salt, cumin, tomato purée and tomatoes. Cook for a few minutes, until the onions and tomatoes are just soft.

3. Now add the jalapeños, the meat-free chicken pieces, the vegetarian mince and the kidney beans and cook for 10 minutes. Add the ketchup and water and cook, covered, for 10 minutes, then add the coriander, stir through and take off the heat.

4. Put the ricotta into a bowl with three-quarters of the Cheddar and mix well.

5. Now start to layer by putting half the chilli mixture into the base of your baking dish. Add 5 of the tortilla quarters, to cover the chilli.

6. Layer half the ricotta mixture over the tortillas and spread evenly.

7. Do the same again with the rest of the tortilla pieces and ricotta, then sprinkle with the rest of the grated Cheddar.

8. Bake in the oven for 30–40 minutes, or until the edges are crisp.

PREP 50 MINUTES

COOK 30 MINUTES

For the chilli

5 tablespoons olive oil

7 cloves of garlic, crushed

1 medium red onion (approx. 120g), roughly chopped

1 teaspoon salt

2 teaspoons ground cumin

1 tablespoon tomato purée

2 medium tomatoes, diced

90g pickled jalapeños, roughly chopped (you can leave these out if you prefer it less spicy)

350g meat-free, chicken-type pieces

350g vegetarian mince

240g kidney beans, drained

8 tablespoons ketchup

150ml water

15g fresh coriander, chopped

For the white sauce

500g ricotta

200g Cheddar cheese, grated (set aside a quarter for the top)

2½ large wholemeal tortillas, quartered

BEEF SKEWERS WITH PUY LENTIL & CHICKPEA SALAD

Serves 4

These are my favourite beef skewers that I cook every year on the barbecue. The recipe has lots of lemon in it, which means the meat doesn't have to sit in the fridge overnight to marinate. Seeing as I never have any room in the fridge, this seemed the best idea. I love these skewers served with a simple fresh lentil and chickpea salad.

PREP 1 HOUR
COOK 10–20 MINUTES

For the beef skewers

4 beef fillet steaks (approx. 600g), very thinly sliced

4 tablespoons olive oil

peeled rind and juice of 2 lemons

2 small green chillies

30g fresh coriander, chopped

1 teaspoon salt

For the salad

1 large clove of garlic, crushed and finely chopped

1 large red onion, diced

15g fresh coriander, finely chopped

1 small chilli, deseeded and finely chopped

1 tablespoon wholegrain mustard

3 tablespoons olive oil

250g cooked Puy lentils (buy a ready-cooked pouch)

2 x 400g tins of chickpeas, drained

juice of 1 lime

¼ teaspoon salt

1. Soak eight wooden skewers in cold water for 15 minutes. This will prevent them burning during cooking.

2. Slice the steak lengthways as thinly as possible and set aside in a bowl.

3. Put the oil, lemon rind, lemon juice, chillies, coriander and salt into a food processor. Blitz to a smooth paste, then add the paste to the bowl of steak pieces. Mix well, then cover and set aside for 20 minutes.

4. Meanwhile, make the salad. Put the garlic, onion, coriander, chilli, mustard and oil into a bowl and mix well. Add the lentils and chickpeas. Squeeze in the lime juice and mix through, then cover and set aside.

5. Preheat the oven to 240°C/220°C fan/gas 9 and lightly grease a roasting dish. Or if you prefer to cook your skewers on a griddle pan, grease it lightly and put it on a medium to high heat to start warming up.

6. Meanwhile, skewer the beef pieces in a zigzag pattern. Do this until you have filled all eight skewers. If you have any leftover marinade, just dab it on top of the beef.

7. Line the skewers on to the greased roasting dish and bake for 8–10 minutes, making sure to turn them over halfway through. Or, if griddling, put them on the hot pan and cook for 3–4 minutes on each side.

8. Once cooked, serve the warm beef skewers with the salad alongside.

Tip: Once the meat has been marinated and skewered, these can be frozen and later cooked straight from frozen.

FIVE-SPICE DUCK PIE

Serves 8–10

Most of my recipes are inspired by a curiosity that keeps me up at night making notes. I often wondered what a cold game pie tasted like, but I couldn't find a halal one that I could actually eat. So I decided to make my own. I was out looking for a goose at Christmas and stumbled upon a wholesaler selling ducks. I asked for 2 duck breasts but came home with 12 frozen ducks! It wasn't easy to explain to my husband why I had 12 ducks, but needless to say, I made a lot of duck pies that year and this is one of them. Duck breast lends itself really well to Chinese five-spice. The blend I use is a mix of star anise, fennel seeds, cinnamon, black pepper and cloves. If you are feeling adventurous, you can make this blend yourself, though it's easy to find similar ones in the spice aisles of most supermarkets.

1. For the filling, put the rashers, duck breasts, onion, coriander, five-spice, peanuts and orange zest into a bowl. Give it all a good mix by hand.

2. Preheat the oven to 180°C/160°C fan/gas 4 and have a 20cm loose-bottomed round tin ready.

3. To make the pastry, put the water into a pan with the fat, then bring to the boil and turn off the heat immediately.

4. Put the flour into a large bowl and make a well in the centre. Add the hot water and fat mixture and mix with a palette knife. The mixture will be hot, so don't get your hands in straight away. Leave for about 5 minutes.

5. Roll out the pastry on a clean surface, then set aside a third. Roll out the larger piece and line the base and sides of the tin with it, making sure to have some overhang. Put all the filling mixture into the tin and pat down.

6. Now roll out the other piece of pastry to make the lid and place it on top. Seal the edges by pressing, then cut off the excess and crimp the edges. Use any leftover pastry to decorate the pie however you wish. Glaze with the beaten egg and cut a slit in the top.

7. Bake for 30 minutes, then take out of the oven and lower the temperature to 160°C/140°C fan/gas 3. Brush the top of the pie with the eggwash again and put back into the oven for 90 minutes.

8. Remove from the oven and leave to cool in the tin for 2 hours, then take out of the tin and leave to chill in the fridge, covered with foil. This is great for a picnic or garden party.

PREP 50 MINUTES, PLUS COOLING
COOK 2 HOURS

For the filling

150g rashers, sliced
(bacon or halal turkey)

750g duck breasts (about 6 breasts), skin off and diced

1 red onion (approx. 110g), diced

15g fresh coriander, chopped

2 heaped teaspoons Chinese five-spice

150g salted peanuts, roughly chopped

zest of 1 orange

For the hot water crust pastry

220ml water

200g vegetable fat or lard

575g plain flour

1 medium egg, beaten

AUBERGINE & FETA TART

Serves 4–6

This simple tart is easy to make and easy to freeze. With the pastry-making stage taken out, it's that much quicker to put together, but of course if you are having a lazy weekend you might want to make the pastry from scratch, in your pyjamas, like I do. (And then I use the extra time while my pastry is chilling to play hide-and-seek or do a jigsaw with the kids!) However, when saving time is the priority, ready-rolled is ideal, and I've opted for easy toppings too. The soft aubergine works really well with the salty feta. I like to cut it up like a pizza and serve it with salad.

PREP 45 MINUTES
COOK 20 MINUTES

2 aubergines (approx. 300g)

100ml olive oil, plus extra for drizzling

salt, for seasoning

4 heaped tablespoons sun-dried tomato paste

2 cloves of garlic, crushed and finely chopped

1 teaspoon dried basil

320g packet of ready-rolled puff pastry

1 small egg, beaten

100g feta cheese

a few leaves of fresh basil

1. Trim the aubergines and slice them lengthways. Brush the slices all over with the olive oil and lightly season. You may need more or less oil depending on the size of your aubergines, as the sizes can vary every time.

2. Place a griddle pan (or a frying pan, if that's all you have) on a medium to high heat. Add a few slices of aubergine and griddle on each side until they become tender. Place on a plate, then do the same with the rest of the aubergine slices.

3. Preheat the oven to 220°C/200°C fan/gas 7.

4. In a small bowl, mix together the tomato paste, garlic and dried basil.

5. Take the pastry out of the fridge and unroll it. It should already be on a piece of baking paper, so leave it there. Place on a large baking tray.

6. Using a small knife, score a 1cm border all the way around the edge of the pastry. Now prick the base of the pastry, avoiding the border – this will stop the inner part of the pastry puffing up. Brush the 1cm border with beaten egg – this will give it a gorgeous sheen when it bakes.

7. Spread the pricked base with all the tomato paste mixture. Lay the aubergine slices all over the tomato paste, then crumble the feta on top.

8. Bake on the middle shelf of the oven for 25–30 minutes.

9. Once baked, take the tart out of the oven and leave on the tray for 10 minutes. Rip up the basil, sprinkle all over the top, and finally give the tart a good drizzle of olive oil.

Photos (inc. finished dish) overleaf →

TOMATO & ARTICHOKE PANZANELLA

Serves 4

I remember watching someone make panzanella on a very popular TV show, where the contestants each host a dinner party for the others in their own home. I watched that show more for the amusing voiceover than for the recipes. This particular cook didn't exactly make soaked stale bread look appealing when he literally turned the mixture into mush. The key here is not to over-soak or over-handle, but to leave it just long enough to get delicious flavour into the dry bread. With the artichokes, tomatoes and fresh basil, this is a delicious combination. It's the kind of dish I would serve as a starter, or as a side with a main, or as a light lunch. I always make a mountain of the stuff for our barbecue table in the summer.

**PREP 20 MINUTES,
PLUS RESTING
NO COOK**

6 anchovy fillets

3 tablespoons balsamic vinegar

100ml olive oil

200g bread (white or brown), in small to medium chunks

600g ripe cherry tomatoes, halved

1 x 400g tin of artichoke hearts (drained weight 240g), quartered

1 tablespoon capers, drained and roughly chopped

1 small red onion, finely sliced

salt and pepper, for seasoning

a large handful of fresh basil, roughly torn

1. Begin by mashing the anchovy fillets in a bowl, using the back of a fork, or in a large pestle and mortar. Mix in the balsamic vinegar and oil, and set aside.

2. Put the bread, tomatoes, artichokes, capers and onion into a large bowl and mix together. Season just lightly and mix again. Using your hands, give the tomatoes a squeeze to release some of their moisture.

3. Drizzle over the balsamic and oil mixture and mix, using your hands so that everything is really well combined.

4. Mix in the basil, then leave it all to soak in for about 30 minutes before serving.

TOMATO & CUCUMBER GAZPACHO

Serves 4

Gazpacho is a delicious 'no cook' soup made with raw vegetables, blitzed up. It's traditionally served cold, in particular during hot summers in Spain and Portugal. That's exactly how I like to eat it too, so during that one week of summer we usually get here in the UK, I will always find an opportunity to make it! It's quick, simple, easy and adaptable. Best of all, it can be made in advance, stored in the fridge, and no cooking is necessary. Which also makes it perfect for lunches on the go.

1. For the garlic you will need a blowtorch or a gas hob. If you don't have either, you can just miss this step out and put the garlic into the bowl peeled and whole.

2. Burn the garlic over a gas flame on the hob, until the outer skin is totally black. You can do the same thing by placing the garlic on a baking tray and using a blowtorch to burn the skin. Put the burnt garlic skin and garlic cloves into a large bowl. This process gives the whole dish a smoky taste.

3. Add the cucumber, red peppers, cornichons, tomatoes, red onion, bread and dried tarragon. Season, and give everything a good mix to combine well. Add the vinegar and oil and mix well, using your hands and making sure to give it all a squeeze.

4. Cover and leave in the fridge for 4 hours, or overnight if you have time.

5. Spoon everything into a regular blender and blitz to a smooth paste. You can use a stick blender, if you have one. If the mixture is too thick, add some olive oil and blitz till you get a runnier consistency.

6. Check the seasoning, then drizzle with a little olive oil and serve with some fresh tarragon sprinkled on top.

**PREP 20 MINUTES,
PLUS CHILLING
NO COOK**

3 cloves of garlic, unpeeled and left whole

1 cucumber (approx. 400g), peeled and chopped

2 red peppers (approx. 300g), deseeded and chopped

180g drained cornichons, roughly chopped

1kg ripe tomatoes, cored and chopped

1 red onion, roughly chopped

75g dried crusty bread, crusts kept on, roughly chopped

4 tablespoons dried tarragon

salt, for seasoning

4 tablespoons apple cider vinegar

100ml olive oil, plus extra to drizzle

fresh tarragon, to serve

HALLOUMI & WATERMELON SKEWERS WITH TAMARIND DIP

Makes 8 skewers

I am obsessed with this tamarind dip and eat it with almost anything. It works really well with different textures and tastes, like these skewers, which are a mixture of crisp bread, sweet juicy watermelon and salty halloumi. In this recipe, I give you a special trick to keep the halloumi lovely and gooey in the centre, so it doesn't dry out during cooking. These skewers are great on the barbecue, but are just as good done indoors on a griddle or under the grill.

**PREP 25 MINUTES,
PLUS SOAKING
COOK 10 MINUTES
(6 MINUTES IF GRIDDLING,
8–10 MINUTES IF GRILLING)**

For the drizzle

75ml olive oil

1 teaspoon onion salt

1 teaspoon garlic powder

1 teaspoon chilli flakes

1 tablespoon dried
fenugreek leaves

For the skewers

500g halloumi cheese, cut
into 2.5cm cubes

400g watermelon, cut into
2.5cm cubes

150g white bread, cut into
2.5cm cubes

For the dip

95g tamarind paste

100ml water

60g runny honey

½ teaspoon ground cinnamon

1 small red onion (approx.
60g), chopped

1. Soak eight wooden skewers in cold water for 15 minutes.

2. Mix the drizzle ingredients in a jug.

3. Put the halloumi into a bowl and boil a kettle of water. Pour the boiling water over the halloumi and leave for 20 minutes. This will make the cheese really soft and smooth in the centre when cooked.

4. Drain the halloumi, then put it into a large bowl with the watermelon and bread. Drizzle over the oil mixture and give everything a good mix.

5. Thread cubes of halloumi, watermelon and bread on to each skewer, about six cubes on each, mixing them up. If there is any oil mixture left in the base of the bowl, drizzle it over the skewers.

6. To make the dip, mix all the ingredients together in a bowl.

7. Place a griddle pan on a high heat. Brush it lightly or spray with a little oil. Put in four skewers at a time and griddle for about 6 minutes, making sure to turn them every 1½ minutes so that you char all sides. If you prefer, you can cook them all at once under the grill, for 8–10 minutes, turning occasionally.

8. Set aside on a plate, with some foil over the top to keep them warm, while you grill the rest of the skewers.

9. Serve with the tamarind dip.

LAMB & MINT PASTIES WITH QUICK APPLE PICKLE

Makes 6 pasties and about 450ml pickle

If I had a pound for every time I've said I wouldn't eat a pasty for lunch all five days in a week, I would be a very rich lady! I not only love eating pasties, I love making them too, since I enjoy the repetition of preparing things, like on a production line. I love the solitude of doing it alone, and equally the mayhem of appointing different jobs to different members of my family, such as roller, cutter, filler, crimper and eggwash brusher. These pasties are one of my favourite types, filled with soft baked lamb, potatoes, apples, peas and mint. Perfect for a picnic, accompanied by this aromatic apple pickle.

PREP 50 MINUTES, PLUS CHILLING
COOK 1 HOUR 15 MINUTES

For the pastry

450g plain flour, plus extra for dusting

1 tablespoon baking powder

½ teaspoon salt

125g unsalted butter, cubed

2 large egg yolks

130–140ml cold water

1 egg, lightly beaten, for glazing

For the filling
(see tip opposite)

300g potatoes, peeled and diced

150g frozen peas, defrosted and drained

1 medium white onion, finely chopped (about 180g)

2 small green apples (about 300g), peeled, cored and chopped

1. First make the pastry. Put the flour, baking powder and salt into a large bowl and mix together. Add the butter and rub with your fingertips until the mixture resembles breadcrumbs, or do this in a food processor to speed things up.

2. Add the egg yolks and stir in, using a palette knife. Then add the water a little at a time, still mixing with your palette knife. Get your hands in and start to bring the dough together. You may not need all the water, so add it gradually until the dough just starts to come together.

3. Flatten the pastry and wrap in cling film, then put into the fridge for 1 hour to chill.

4. Meanwhile, make the filling: put the potatoes, peas, onions, apples, lamb, mint and salt into a large bowl and mix together really well. Stir in the melted butter, then add the flour and mix until well incorporated. This will thicken any liquid in the pasties as they bake.

5. Preheat the oven to 180°C/160°C fan/gas 4. Line two trays with baking paper and set aside.

6. Take the pastry out of the fridge and roll out on a floured surface to a thickness of 3-4mm. Use an 18cm round dinner plate as a template, cutting around it with a sharp knife to create six pastry circles. The circles may shrink a little after cutting – if this happens, gently re-roll them to 18cm.

7. Take one of the circles and place the filling on one side, making sure you leave enough to fill the other five. Brush the edge of one half of the circle with beaten egg, then fold over the other half and you should have something that looks like a D shape. Crimp the edges using the tip of a fork or the back of a knife.

8. Make a hole in the top to allow some air to escape and place on the lined tray. Now do the same with the other five circles. Brush all over with the beaten egg and bake in the oven for 50 minutes. Take out of the oven and leave to stand for at least 10 minutes before eating.

9. While the pasties are baking, get started on the apple pickle. Put the oil into a non-stick pan and place on a low heat. Add the mustard seeds, and as soon as they begin to pop, add all the other spices (garlic, ginger, turmeric, fenugreek, chillies, asafoetida and onion seeds). Cook for a few minutes. You don't want to burn any of the spices, so be very careful.

10. Now stir in the vinegar, sugar and salt. Add the apples and water and cook gently for about 20 minutes, until the apples have mostly broken down. You may find some pieces that haven't, but that's fine.

11. Leave to cool in the pan, then serve with the pasties. Transfer the rest of the pickle to a clean jar and refrigerate. It can be kept for up to a month in the fridge.

Tip: When preparing the filling, make sure all the fruit and veg are chopped to roughly the same size, as this helps it all to cook evenly.

300g boneless lamb (leg is ideal), chopped

2 tablespoons dried mint

1 teaspoon salt

40g butter, melted

2 tablespoons plain flour

For the apple pickle

5 tablespoons olive oil

1 teaspoon brown mustard seeds

1 teaspoon garlic granules

½ teaspoon ground ginger

¼ teaspoon ground turmeric

½ teaspoon fenugreek seeds

2 fresh green chillies, thinly sliced

¼ teaspoon asafoetida

½ teaspoon onion seeds

2 tablespoons apple cider vinegar

1 teaspoon caster sugar

½ teaspoon salt

4 green apples, cored and chopped (skin kept on)

200ml water

COUNTRY BEANS

Serves 4

Who doesn't love baked beans? A favourite with kids and grown-ups alike, as an emergency supper, comfort food on toast, part of your morning fry-up, or on the side of chicken and chips, they are a British classic if ever there was one. This recipe takes baked beans to a new level, with more colour, some gentle spices and slightly deeper flavours than the canned ones we know and love. A bowlful of these makes a warm, filling lunch. They also go well with my cheese scones on page 138, if you want something extra alongside.

PREP 15 MINUTES
COOK 35 MINUTES

2 tablespoons olive oil

1 medium red onion, diced

salt and pepper, for seasoning

1 yellow pepper, deseeded and diced

1–2 tablespoons green jalapeños from a jar, drained (add more, to taste)

2 cloves of garlic, finely chopped

1 teaspoon ground cumin

1 teaspoon sweet smoked paprika

1 bay leaf

2 x 400g tins of mixed beans in water, e.g. a mixture of kidney, cannellini and pinto beans, drained

5 medium tomatoes, chopped

1 tablespoon Worcestershire sauce

1 teaspoon Dijon mustard

3 tablespoons chopped fresh coriander leaves

1. Heat a heavy-based medium to large saucepan over a medium heat. Once hot, add a glug of oil and the diced onion. Season with a little salt and pepper and cook until the onion is completely softened and translucent (about 10 minutes), adding the diced pepper after 5 minutes. Turn the heat down a little if necessary as you cook.

2. Add the jalapeños, garlic, cumin, smoked paprika and bay leaf and continue to cook for a further 2 minutes, or until everything is fragrant but not burning.

3. Stir in the beans and tomatoes, along with the Worcestershire sauce and mustard. Bring to a simmer, then reduce the heat, cover, and allow to simmer gently for 20 minutes, stirring lightly now and again, until the tomatoes have collapsed a little and the beans have softened. Take off the lid for the last 5 minutes to help the sauce thicken.

4. Remove from the heat and gently stir in the chopped coriander. Serve while warm.

BREADED MACKEREL IN TZATZIKI PITTAS

Serves 2

I love fish and chips, but I prefer to do the frying myself, rather than buying from a takeaway. It's easy and it makes me feel better about what I'm eating. My husband once went fishing with friends off the coast of Wales and came home proudly with his prized catch. This meal was the outcome. I really enjoy the contrast of the crumbs around the oily mackerel flesh, which makes a welcome change from cod. It's great in toasted pittas with crisp lettuce. Serve with my homemade tzatziki, which has a spicy kick from the addition of fried cumin seeds.

1. To make the tzatziki, put the yoghurt into a bowl with the cucumber, garlic, chopped mint and dill, then stir in the lemon juice.

2. Heat the oil gently in a small pan. Add the cumin seeds and warm through, being careful not to burn them. Once you hear the first pop, take the pan off the heat and straight away add the seeds to the yoghurt mixture. Stir through and set aside.

3. Put the beaten egg on one rimmed plate and the breadcrumbs on another.

4. Dip one of the mackerel fillets into the egg mixture. Take out, season on both sides, then dip into the breadcrumbs, making sure to cover both sides of the fillet well. Press the crumbs on to the fish. Do the same with the other piece of fish.

5. Put the oil into a non-stick frying pan and place on a medium heat.

6. Add the fish and cook on one side for 4 minutes, then turn over and cook for 4 minutes on the other side. Place on kitchen paper to drain.

7. Toast the pitta breads and slice each one along the long edge to create a pocket. Add the lettuce and mackerel, and top with the tzatziki. Serve any extra tzatziki on the side.

PREP 30 MINUTES
COOK 10 MINUTES

For the tzatziki

150g Greek yoghurt

½ a cucumber (150g), peeled, cored and diced

3 cloves of garlic, finely chopped

1 large sprig of fresh mint, finely chopped

2 sprigs of fresh dill, finely chopped

juice of ½ a lemon

2 tablespoons olive oil

1 teaspoon cumin seeds

For the breaded mackerel

2 mackerel fillets (approx. 240g), skin on

salt, for seasoning

1 medium egg, lightly beaten

50g dried breadcrumbs

5 tablespoons olive oil

8 leaves of little gem lettuce, thinly sliced

2 pitta breads

Midweek Meals

The mad midweek meals are the ones that can make me or break me! If I can go a full week and manage the meals without falling apart completely, well, that for me is an achievement. It was very different back before life got hectic. Then, I could leisurely cook my dinner while dipping in and out of ironing, texting, talking to my sister on the phone . . . oh, and drinking cups and cups of Yorkshire tea. But eating and feeding has changed over the years. These days, things are busy enough without worrying about what we're going to eat. Mealtimes are no longer just about nurture, they are also about being thrifty, being inventive, being creative, and most of all, cooking something that causes everyone to make yummy sounds and keeps them going till the weekend.

LAMB BHUNA WITH GARLIC NAAN

Serves 4

Much as I love a home-cooked curry, I needed a faster way of making them. So this is my speedy curry solution, with a sauce that gets blitzed in a food processor before being cooked. It's sweet, aromatic and very quick, letting you enjoy the curry and some free time. Even better, every element of the dish can be frozen, saving you even more time on another day.

**PREP 40 MINUTES,
PLUS RESTING
COOK 1 HOUR**

For the lamb bhuna

200ml olive oil

2 teaspoons salt

10 cloves of garlic, peeled

50g ginger, peeled and sliced

4 small onions (approx. 400g), roughly chopped

2 large peppers (approx. 400g), roughly chopped

4 large red chillies, roughly chopped

1 teaspoon cinnamon

1 teaspoon turmeric

4 teaspoons curry powder

100ml water

800g lamb leg, diced

300ml water

15g fresh coriander, chopped

For the naan

200g self-raising flour, plus extra for dusting

2 tablespoons garlic granules

1 teaspoon sugar

1 teaspoon salt

25g unsalted butter, softened

50g unsalted butter, melted

1. First make the curry paste. Put the olive oil, salt, garlic, ginger, onions, peppers, chillies, cinnamon, turmeric, curry powder and 100ml of water into a food processor. Blitz the whole lot to a smooth paste and put to one side.

2. Next make the dough for the naan. Put the flour, garlic granules, sugar, salt and softened butter into a bowl. Mix everything together well and rub in the butter.

3. Make a well in the centre and add the water. Mix with a palette knife, then get your hands in and bring the dough together.

4. On a floured work surface, knead the dough for 10 minutes by hand, or 5 minutes if using a mixer.

5. Wrap the dough in cling film and leave on the worktop to rest for 20 minutes.

6. While the dough is resting, start cooking the curry. Place a pan on a medium heat and add half the curry paste. (Put the other half of the paste into a jar and store in the freezer, ready for the next time you need a curry hit.)

7. Cook the curry paste for 10 minutes. Add the lamb and cook for another 10 minutes.

8. Add 200ml of water and leave the bhuna to simmer gently for 30 minutes with the lid on.

9. While the bhuna is simmering, divide the naan dough into four equal pieces and roll each one out to the thickness of a pound coin.

10. Put a griddle pan on a high heat. Put one of your naans on the griddle and cook for 3 minutes on each side. Cover with foil and keep warm while you griddle the rest of the naans.

11. Once the bhuna is cooked, take it off the heat and add the chopped coriander. Brush the warm naans with melted butter on both sides and serve with the bhuna.

SPICED BEAN & BANGER STEW

Serves 4

Sausages didn't used to be something that was widely available to people following a halal diet. So I never really got introduced to them until just over a decade ago. Oh, and what an introduction it was! I remember the first month, the honeymoon period, when I'd have a Full English for breakfast, a sausage and egg sandwich for lunch, toad-in-the-hole for dinner and cold leftover sausages from the fridge when I was peckish doing the midnight breastfeed. Since then, I have reined it in, but I still love a good sausage and bean stew. One pot, simple and hearty.

1. Use a large casserole or heavy-based pan and place on a medium heat. Add the chunks of sausage and cook, stirring occasionally, making sure they are fully cooked through. This should take only about 10 minutes.

2. Take the sausage pieces out of the pan, leaving the pan on the heat and setting the sausage aside in a bowl.

3. Add the olive oil and garlic to the pan and cook for a few minutes. Now add the celery, red onions, tomato purée, carrots, salt and tomatoes. Cook on a medium heat for 12–15 minutes.

4. Add the paprika and cinnamon to the sauce and let the spices cook for 5 minutes.

5. Add the beans, water and the cooked sausage, put the lid on the pan, and cook on a medium to low heat for 45–50 minutes.

6. Once cooked through, the whole stew will have thickened significantly.

7. Take off the heat and stir in the chopped parsley.

PREP 25 MINUTES
COOK 1 HOUR 20 MINUTES

6 sausages (400g pack),
cut into chunks

50ml olive oil

4 cloves of garlic, finely
chopped

3 celery stalks, sliced
(approx. 100g)

3 small red onion (approx.
300g), finely chopped

2 tablespoons tomato purée

2 carrots (approx. 140g),
thinly sliced

1 teaspoon salt

2 tomatoes, chopped
(approx. 200g)

1 teaspoon paprika

1 teaspoon ground cinnamon

3 x 400g tins of butter beans
(235g drained weight per tin),
drained and rinsed

500ml water
(or chicken stock)

a handful of fresh parsley
(15g), finely chopped

OYSTER MUSHROOM &
SOBA NOODLE SOUP

Serves 4

Who doesn't love a noodle soup? It's an easy way to give leftover vegetables another lease of life, by serving them in hot brothy goodness. I like to use soba (or buckwheat) noodles, which have a distinct dark colour and really keep their bite despite being cooked in the liquid. This simple broth is flavoured with miso, to give it a sweetness, and with a hint of kaffir lime for its aroma. I tend to make this with just vegetables, but you can easily add shredded chicken to it, if you like.

PREP 15 MINUTES
COOK 15 MINUTES

1.5 litres vegetable stock

5cm ginger (approx. 50g), peeled and finely chopped

3 cloves of garlic, peeled and finely chopped

5 tablespoons dark soy sauce

2 teaspoons runny honey

1 teaspoon chilli flakes

1 tablespoon white miso paste

150g oyster mushrooms, any large ones roughly torn up

125g buckwheat noodles

3 spring onions, finely sliced

1 x 225g tin of bamboo shoots (drained weight 125g), sliced into thin strips

5 dried kaffir lime leaves, crushed in your hand

juice of 1 lime

a large handful of fresh coriander, roughly chopped

1. Put the stock into a large pan and bring to the boil. As soon as it boils, turn the heat down almost completely and leave it at a gentle simmer.

2. Add the ginger, garlic, soy sauce, honey, chilli flakes, miso paste and mushrooms. Leave to simmer for about 5 minutes, then add the noodles, giving them a stir so that they are dispersed through the stock. If they sit together in a clump, they will stick.

3. Turn the heat up, bring to the boil, and cook the noodles for 6 minutes.

4. Lower the heat almost completely again, then stir in the spring onions, bamboo shoots, kaffir lime leaves, lime juice and coriander.

5. Leave to simmer for a few minutes, just to warm the bamboo shoots, then take off the heat and serve.

SMOKED HADDOCK RAREBIT WITH CHICORY & RADISH SALAD

Serves 4

Welsh rarebit is essentially a very fancy version of cheese on toast. It's the best kind, the kind made with careful precision, and everyone who is anyone has their own favourite way of making and eating it. In my recipe I like to flavour the cheese topping with mustard and Worcestershire sauce, and to mix in some poached smoked haddock for a little something extra. Pour it all over toasted slices of fresh bread, top with extra cheese and stick under the grill for rarebit perfection. The salad adds a little freshness on the side.

1. Preheat a grill to a medium high heat. If you don't have access to a grill, preheat the oven to 200°C/180°C fan/gas 6.

2. On a medium heat, place a frying pan just big enough to fit the haddock. Put the haddock into the pan, skin side up, and pour over the milk. Bring to a gentle simmer, then let the fish poach for 2–3 minutes. Remove the fish from the pan, reserving the milk.

3. Once cool enough to handle, peel off the skin and flake the fish into a bowl, in large chunks. Keep warm under cling film.

4. To prepare the salad, mix together the oil, mustard and lemon juice until combined. Season with salt and pepper. Slice the radishes and separate the chicory leaves, tearing any large ones.

5. Meanwhile, heat the butter in a small, heavy-based pan over a medium heat. Once melted, add the flour and stir in, cooking for 4–5 minutes or until the mixture resembles ground almonds. Whisk in the reserved poaching milk, bit by bit, until completely combined, then cook gently for 3–4 minutes, until fairly thick.

6. Add the Worcestershire sauce, mustard and three-quarters of the Cheddar and stir until the cheese has melted. Season as necessary. Remove from the heat and whisk in the egg yolk.

7. Toast the bread until golden on both sides, then put the slices of toast on a baking tray. Gently stir the flaked haddock into the rarebit sauce and divide between the pieces of toast. Top with the remaining cheese.

8. Place under the preheated grill for 2–3 minutes, or until dark golden in colour. Alternatively, cook the rarebit in the hot oven for 10–15 minutes until golden.

9. Meanwhile, mix the salad with the dressing and season if you like. Serve with the hot rarebit.

PREP 15 MINUTES
COOK 20 MINUTES

For the rarebit

2 x 150g undyed smoked haddock fillets, skin on, bones removed

400ml whole milk

25g butter

25g plain flour

1 teaspoon Worcestershire sauce

1 teaspoon wholegrain mustard

75g mature Cheddar chesse, grated

salt and pepper, for seasoning

1 egg yolk

4 large thick slices of bread (e.g. sourdough or bloomer)

For the salad

4–5 tablespoons hazelnut oil

2 teaspoons wholegrain mustard

juice of ½ a lemon, or to taste

1 large handful of radishes, trimmed and thinly sliced

2 heads of chicory, thinly sliced

FENUGREEK PARATHAS

Serves 6

These parathas are an homage to those mashed potato lovers who always make too much mash. I always make too much mash, my sister always makes too much mash, and we all spend an afternoon trying to work out what to do with the leftovers. Well, this is a great way to savour that extra mash, and using a block of ready-made puff pastry lets you make the easiest fenugreek parathas ever. Served with cool yoghurt and a mango pickle, they make a simple but delicious meal.

PREP 30 MINUTES
COOK 35 MINUTES

250g leftover mashed potato (see tip below)

2 spring onions, finely chopped

½ teaspoon salt

1 teaspoon chilli flakes

2 tablespoons dried fenugreek leaves

500g ready-made puff pastry

plain flour, for dusting

100g melted butter

Greek yoghurt and mango pickle, to serve

1. Put the mashed potato into a bowl and add the spring onions, salt, chilli flakes and fenugreek leaves. Mix it all up so it is all well combined.

2. Divide the mixture into six equal amounts and set aside.

3. Divide your puff pastry into six equal pieces. One at a time, roll each piece of pastry into a ball, then flatten so it's wide enough to house the potato filling.

4. Place one-sixth of the filling on the flattened pastry and encase within the pastry.

5. Flour your work surface very lightly. Place the stuffed pastry seam-side down on the work surface and roll out. Make sure to turn it so you get a good circle. Aim for a diameter of about 18cm and a thickness of about 3mm.

6. Repeat the same for the other five pieces of pastry. If you are doing other things, or if the pastry starts to get sticky, place the rolled-out parathas in the fridge, separated by sheets of greaseproof paper.

7. Heat a large frying pan (preferably non-stick) over a medium heat. In batches, place the parathas in the hot pan and cook for 2–3 minutes on both sides.

8. Take off the heat and brush the parathas with butter. Serve warm with the yoghurt and pickle.

Tip: To make 250g of mash, cook 1 large (300g) potato in the microwave for 10–15 minutes in 5-minute bursts, then peel off the skin and mash the flesh.

CLOVE & SQUASH RISOTTO

Serves 4

I'm certainly no expert at cooking risotto but I do love making it. It's a little more time-consuming than other rice dishes, but the finished dish is well worth the wait. Risotto is all about standing in front of the stove and watching your dish as it transforms, and this recipe is no different. The sweet squash is complemented by the addition of ground cloves, mixed with the slow-cooked risotto grains and the tang of Parmesan. It's the perfect opportunity to stand at the stove and have a chat on the phone to someone whom you haven't spoken to for a while.

PREP 20 MINUTES
COOK 30 MINUTES

2 tablespoons olive oil, plus a drizzle, to garnish

½ a small butternut squash, peeled and cubed (approx. 300g prepped weight)

¼ teaspoon ground cloves

½ teaspoon salt

1.75 litres vegetable stock

50g unsalted butter

1 small onion (approx. 150g), finely chopped

350g risotto rice

70g Parmesan, finely grated

a handful of rocket, to garnish

1. Place a frying pan on a medium heat and add the oil. When the oil has warmed up, add the squash, followed by the ground cloves and salt, and cook gently for 15–20 minutes, until the squash has softened.

2. Meanwhile, put the stock into a pan on the hob and bring to the boil. Once it has boiled, leave it to simmer.

3. To make the risotto you will need a wide non-stick pan. Place it on a medium heat and add the butter.

4. Once the butter has melted, go ahead and add the chopped onion and cook for about 5 minutes, till it is soft but not browned.

5. Now add the risotto rice. Cook on a high heat for 2 minutes, then turn the heat back down to medium.

6. Add a ladle of the hot stock to the rice and stir until all the liquid has been absorbed. Keep doing this until the rice is soft but still has a little bite in the middle. This should take about 18–20 minutes. But it's the perfect time for a catch-up. Get on that blower!

7. Once all the stock has been added and the rice is soft, stir in the cooked squash.

8. Add the grated Parmesan and mix through. If the risotto has stiffened too much, add a splash more stock to loosen it a little.

9. Check the seasoning and garnish the risotto with rocket leaves and olive oil.

GARAM MASALA RICE & PEAS WITH RUNNY FRIED EGGS

Serves 4

This recipe is the ethnic version of egg and chips. We almost always have a Tupperware full of this rice in the freezer. I usually cook it en masse, giving me the excuse to freeze batches, so we can later whip it out, warm it up and fry a quick egg to go with it. The rice is lightly fragrant with spices and has a gorgeous brown colour from the caramelized onions. This meal is a firm favourite in our household, and once you've tried this recipe I assure you that you will feel like a rice pro! I certainly did after learning this one.

1. Soak the rice in cold water and set aside.

2. Put the clarified butter into a large non-stick pan and place on a high heat. Once the butter has melted, add the onions and turn the heat down to medium. Let the onions cook – at this point don't be tempted to stir them.

3. You will see that the onions will start browning at the edges of the pan to begin with, so now stir and bring these brown onions to the centre. Keep doing this until all the onions are brown. This can take about 15–20 minutes. The onions should be almost black, not burnt but a very dark brown. Take them off the heat and let the butter cool down for about 10 minutes.

4. Now add 250ml of boiling water and put the pan back on the heat. The onions will slowly soften as the water evaporates.

5. You will know the onions are ready when you squeeze a piece between the back of your spoon and the inside of the pan and the onion disintegrates. At this point, add the salt, garam masala and frozen peas. Cook for 3–5 minutes.

6. Drain the rice and stir into the onion mix.

7. Now add the remaining 750ml of boiling water, stir, and leave to boil for 15 minutes. Once all the water has evaporated, lower the temperature as much as you can and put a lid on the pan. Leave to steam for 10 minutes with the lid on.

8. Meanwhile, fry the eggs. Put the oil into a pan on a medium heat. Crack in the eggs and cook on one side for 3 minutes, basting the tops with oil from the pan to cook the whites.

9. Serve the hot rice with the warm runny egg.

PREP 15 MINUTES
COOK 1 HOUR 10 MINUTES

300g basmati rice

100g clarified butter (ghee), or, if you can't find this, unsalted butter

1 small onion (approx. 150g), sliced

1 litre boiling water

1 teaspoon salt

4 teaspoons garam masala

150g frozen peas

4 tablespoons olive oil

4 eggs, for frying

PRAWN & ORANGE CURRY
WITH BASMATI RICE

Serves 3

Someone once said to me, 'Fish and fruit don't go together.' But I think you will find that they do! Or at least that's what my Nan led me to believe for a very long time, and boy, was she right. Although I grew up in a home where fruit and freshwater fish were considered a winning combo, I'm always slightly deterred by people's hesitation at the very thought of the two together. But I do love a challenge, and every time I get that reaction I set out to change perceptions – and this dish will do exactly that. What your mind doesn't comprehend, your taste buds will make sense of. I promise. Just let me prove you wrong.

PREP 20 MINUTES
COOK 25 MINUTES

**For the prawn and
orange curry**

3 tablespoons olive oil

3 cloves of garlic, finely
chopped

1 small onion (approx. 75g),
chopped

1 small green chilli, chopped

¼ teaspoon turmeric

½ teaspoon salt, plus more
for seasoning

1 teaspoon ground cumin

2 teaspoon paprika

200ml water

zest and juice of 1 large
orange

300g raw shelled tiger prawns

a handful of fresh coriander
(approx. 15g), chopped

For the basmati rice

225g basmati rice

500ml cold water

1. Put the olive oil in a pan and place on a medium heat. Add the crushed garlic and cook for a minute.

2. Add the chopped onion and green chilli and cook for a further 3 minutes, allowing the onions to soften.

3. Stir in the turmeric, salt, cumin and paprika. The dish will be very dry now because of the spices, so add the water. Then add the orange zest and juice, stir again, and allow the whole thing to cook gently for about 12–15 minutes.

4. While the sauce is simmering, let's move on to the rice. Place the rice in a medium pan so the grains have room to move while boiling. Add the water and bring to the boil over a high heat, stirring after 5 minutes. Let it boil for another 5 minutes and then stir again. The water should have almost entirely evaporated.

5. Put the pan on the lowest setting on your hob, cover and leave to steam for 5 minutes.

6. The curry sauce should now have reduced and thickened. Check the seasoning, then go ahead and add your prawns. Cook for as little as 3-4 minutes or just until they have gone pink.

7. Take off the heat and stir in the coriander. Serve the curry with the hot rice.

IMAM BAYILDI WITH LEMON COUSCOUS

Serves 4

This is a typically Turkish dish. There are many variations out there and this is my addition to the world's repertoire of imam bayildi recipes. My sister has an addiction to aubergine. I don't often use the world addiction lightly, but she called me once and said she had great news. Now imagine my excitement: New baby? New house? New job? No. She said, 'I've bought a whole box of aubergines for a pound! I'm going to cook aubergines all week!' She genuinely will eat aubergine three times a week, and she is always pleased when I cook my version of imam bayildi for her, to add a fourth aubergine dish to her weekly quota. While you enjoy this recipe, I will be seeking an Aubergine Anonymous Addiction Association for her.

1. Place a large frying pan on a medium heat and add the oil.

2. Once the oil is hot, add the onions, salt and tomatoes. Cook for about 3 minutes, until the onions have softened slightly and the tomatoes have softened and started to break down.

3. Now add the cinnamon and cumin and cook for about a minute. Add the aubergines, and stir for 1–2 minutes. The mixture will start to stick to the pan a little because of the dry spices, so add the water and continue to cook on a low to medium heat for 10–15 minutes, until the aubergines are tender.

4. Meanwhile, place the couscous in a large bowl. Bring the stock to a boil and add the zest and juice of the lemon. Now pour the stock over the couscous. Stir, then cover with cling film.

5. Leave for 10 minutes, then uncover and use a fork to fluff up the couscous. Check the seasoning and stir in a little of the chopped parsley.

6. Serve the couscous and imam bayildi together, and top the aubergine with parsley and toasted almonds.

PREP 20 MINUTES
COOK 20 MINUTES

For the imam bayildi

100ml olive oil

3 red onions (approx. 450g), cut into large chunks

½ teaspoon salt

4 large tomatoes (approx. 400g), cut into large chunks

1 teaspoon ground cinnamon

2 teaspoons ground cumin

2 large aubergines (approx. 400g), cut into small (2cm) chunks

150ml water

a handful of fresh flat-leaf parsley (approx. 15g), chopped

25g toasted flaked almonds

For the couscous

200g couscous

250ml vegetable stock

zest and juice of 1 lemon

salt, for seasoning

TANDOORI COD BURGER

Serves 2

Everyone loves a bright piece of nuclear tandoori chicken, right? I have been known to dabble in synthetic flavours and colourings like the best of them, but even I can't get my head round food colouring for chicken! Luckily, there are alternative ways of colouring food naturally, using simple ground spices that not only impart flavour, but also produce beautiful colours that are enhanced with cooking. This tandoori cod is tinted with a masala mix that contains ground tomato powder. The fish is cooked gently, then served with a zingy onion and cucumber salad, all sandwiched between slices of brioche. Not a dyed pink finger in sight!

PREP 15 MINUTES
COOK 6 MINUTES

4 tablespoons olive oil

1½ tablespoons tandoori masala

3 tablespoons Greek yoghurt

salt, for seasoning

2 pieces of skinless cod fillet (approx. 100g each)

¼ of a red onion (approx. 35g), thinly sliced

5 fresh mint leaves, thinly sliced

100g cucumber, centre core removed and the rest sliced

4 slices of brioche

1. Put 2 tablespoons of oil, the tandoori masala, 1 tablespoon of Greek yoghurt and the salt into a medium bowl and stir to combine.

2. Add the cod to the bowl and coat with the masala mix.

3. Put a small frying pan on a medium heat and add the remaining 2 tablespoons of oil. Once it's hot, turn the heat down slightly and add the cod. Cook gently for 2–3 minutes on either side, then take off the heat and set aside, covered with foil.

4. Put the red onion, mint leaves and cucumber into another bowl and mix together, seasoning to taste.

5. Spread the rest of the Greek yoghurt over two slices of the brioche. Pile half the cucumber salad on to each slice. Top each one with the tandoori cod and close the sandwiches with the remaining two brioche slices.

STEAK & KIDNEY RAS-EL-HANOUT PIE

Serves 4

With its soft steamed pie crust, earthy spices and strong steak and kidney flavours, this pie is more satisfying than most, especially midweek when you need something to keep you going until Friday. Every corner of the world has its own special spice blend that evolves with time, and ras el hanout is a North African blend, usually a combination of cardamom, cumin, clove, cinnamon, nutmeg, mace, allspice and turmeric. Other spice blends work here too, so find the one you like most and feel free to experiment with it.

PREP 1 HOUR,
PLUS COOLING
COOK 2 HOURS 45 MINUTES

For the filling

140g lamb's kidney, chopped into small pieces

200ml whole milk

3 tablespoons olive oil

2 cloves of garlic, crushed

5cm fresh ginger, peeled and crushed

1 medium onion, roughly chopped

1 teaspoon salt

400g beef steak (e.g. braising steak), cut into small chunks

300g chestnut mushrooms, cut into small chunks (same size as beef pieces)

4 teaspoons ras el hanout

150ml ginger beer

3 spring onions, finely chopped

For the suet pastry

350g self-raising flour

75g unsalted butter

100g suet

150ml cold water

1. Put the kidney in a bowl, pour in the milk, stir and set aside.

2. Heat the oil in a large non-stick pan on a medium heat. Add the garlic, ginger, onion and salt and cook for 5–10 minutes, until soft. If it starts to stick, don't be tempted to take the pan off the heat. Just add a little water and help it to come away.

3. Now add the steak and cook until the meat is brown. Add the mushrooms and cook for 10 minutes.

4. Drain the kidney and rinse under cold water. Add to the pan and cook for 10 minutes, then stir in the ras el hanout and cook for 5 more minutes before pouring in the ginger beer.

5. Cook for 10–15 minutes more, until all reduced down. Take off the heat, stir in the spring onions and leave to cool completely.

6. Preheat the oven to 190°C/170°C fan/gas 5 and boil a full kettle of water. Grease a 23 x 13cm loaf tin.

7. Start on the pastry by putting the flour, butter and suet into a bowl. Rub with your fingertips until it resembles breadcrumbs. Make a well in the centre, add the water and bring the dough together. Set a third of it aside.

8. Roll the larger piece of pastry to a rectangle of 40 x 30cm, large enough to line the tin with some overhang. Line the tin, leaving the excess pastry attached. Spoon in the cooled pie filling.

9. Roll out the rest of the pastry and place it on top, cutting it to just cover the filling. Trim the overhang, using the sides of the tin as a guide, and fold over the edges, working all the way round.

10. Place a lightly greased rectangle of baking paper over the top of the pie. Cover with foil, then sit the loaf tin in a large roasting tin. Pour boiling water into the roasting tin, to come halfway up the outside of the loaf tin, and steam in the oven for 2 hours.

11. Take out of the oven and transfer to a plate. Serve the pie with mashed potatoes.

RED SPLIT LENTILS
WITH FIVE-SPICE SODA BREAD

Serves 4

This is one of the first recipes I was ever taught. Lentils can be tricky because sometimes they need an overnight soak. Too many times I've forgotten to soak them the night before and had to abandon the recipe. But here they need no soaking and very little attention, they simply like to sit and stew as the flavours enhance. I've served them with an even simpler five-spice soda bread, with absolutely no proving or kneading required. It may just be the most chilled-out meal you have ever made.

1. To get started on the soda bread, preheat the oven to 200°C/180°C fan/gas 6 and line a baking tray with baking paper.

2. Put the flours, salt, bicarbonate of soda and five-spice into a large bowl and give it all a good mix. Make a well in the centre and add a little over half the buttermilk. Bring the dough together by hand, adding more of the buttermilk if needed.

3. As soon as all the flour is absorbed and the dough comes together, lightly flour the work surface, tip the dough on to it and roll it into a neat ball shape. Place on the baking tray.

4. Using a sharp knife, make a cut down the centre vertically and then the same horizontally to form a cross, making sure to cut all the way down to the base.

5. Bake on the middle shelf for 30 minutes, until the bread is golden and sounds hollow when tapped on the base. Put on a wire rack to cool.

6. Meanwhile, rinse the lentils till the water runs clear. Put them in a pan with the cold water, bay leaf, red chilli, turmeric and salt. Bring to the boil and leave to simmer for 30 minutes till the mixture is thicker and the lentils have broken up.

7. Put the butter into a small frying pan and let it melt on a medium heat. Add the sliced garlic and fry until golden. Pour the garlic and butter into the lentils and mix through.

8. Now add the chopped coriander and take the pan off the heat. Serve the warm lentils with chunks of soda bread.

Tip: If you don't have buttermilk, (as most of us normally don't!) just mix 4 tablespoons of lemon juice or white vinegar with 400ml of milk, stir and leave to sit for 5 minutes.

PREP 25 MINUTES,
PLUS COOLING
COOK 1 HOUR 10 MINUTES

For the soda bread

250g plain flour, plus extra for dusting

250 strong bread flour

1 teaspoon salt

1 teaspoon bicarbonate of soda

1 tablespoon Indian five-spice (cumin, mustard, fenugreek, nigella and fennel seeds)

up to 400ml buttermilk (see tip below)

For the lentils

150g red split lentils

1 litre cold water

1 bay leaf

1 dried red chilli

½ teaspoon turmeric

½ teaspoon salt

100g unsalted butter

5 cloves of garlic, sliced thinly

a handful of fresh coriander (approx. 10g), chopped

STICKY STAR ANISE WINGS
WITH CHUNKY CHIPS

Serves 4

I was born and raised in Luton, which is famed for 'chicken, chips and chilli sauce'. I never ate those (or indeed any kind of takeaway) while growing up, but as soon as I turned 18, I discovered freedom, fear and (my parents' worst nightmare) fast food! Chicken and chips are a prized combination, so I decided to make my own version, and here it is. These wings are soft, sticky and certainly finger-licking good. Forget cutlery; your hands are all you need here!

PREP 25 MINUTES
COOK 1 HOUR 10 MINUTES

For the wings

1kg chicken wings, wing tips removed

4 tablespoons brown sauce

4 cloves of garlic, crushed

3 tablespoons light brown sugar

4 tablespoons sweet chilli sauce

4 tablespoons soy sauce

1 tablespoon ground star anise (see tip below)

2 spring onions, thinly sliced (optional)

For the chunky chips

20g salt, plus more for seasoning

1kg large potatoes (about 4-5), peeled and cut into chunky chips

2 litres vegetable oil

1. Find a pan big enough to fit the chicken wings comfortably with some space. Half fill with water and bring to the boil. When boiling, drop the chicken wings in and boil for 15 minutes.

2. Drain the wings and leave to cool. Once cool enough to handle, pat them dry individually, making sure to get rid of all moisture.

3. Clean out the pan, refill with cold water and add the salt. Add the potato chunks, place the pan on a high heat and boil for 4-5 minutes, until tender but not breaking up. Drain the potatoes, spread them out on a tray, then set aside to cool down and dry.

4. Preheat the oven to 180°C/160°C fan/gas 4. Put the brown sauce, garlic, brown sugar, chilli sauce, soy sauce and star anise into a large bowl and mix together. Add the chicken wings and turn them around to coat them with the sauce.

5. Transfer the wings to one large baking tray or two medium trays, keeping them in one even layer. Roast on the middle shelf of the oven for 35-40 minutes, turning the wings after 20 minutes.

6. Meanwhile (about 20 minutes before the wings are done), put the oil in a large deep pan and begin to heat on a high heat. Drop a piece of potato into the oil and as soon as it starts to bubble, sizzle and float, you are ready to add the rest of the potato pieces. If you have a probe thermometer, this should be at about 180°C.

7. Fry the chips for 6-8 minutes - they should be golden brown. Use a slotted spoon to drain them, and place them on a plate lined with kitchen paper. Sprinkle with salt.

8. Serve the hot wings and chips straight away. You can sprinkle thinly sliced spring onion on top of the wings, if you like.

Tip: If you can't find ground star anise, you can grind four whole ones with a pestle and mortar or spice grinder, then sieve to remove any bits.

BLACK BEAN MOLE ENCHILADAS

Serves 6

PREP 30 MINUTES

COOK 1 HOUR 10 MINUTES

For the enchiladas

2–3 tablespoons vegetable oil

1 bay leaf

1 cinnamon stick

1 small onion, chopped

1 celery stick, sliced

1 teaspoon salt

1 large red chilli, chopped

1 tablespoon tomato purée

1 teaspoon each of ground cumin, ground coriander and chilli powder

1 x 400g tin of chopped tomatoes

3 x 400g tins of black beans, drained

large handful fresh coriander

6 tortilla wraps

1 small red onion, thinly sliced

150g Cheddar, finely grated

For the mole sauce

2 tablespoons olive oil

2 cloves of garlic, chopped

1 small onion, chopped

½ teaspoon salt

1 teaspoon each of ground cumin and ground coriander

1 x 400g tin of chopped tomatoes

100g jalapeños, drained

100ml water

4 cubes of 70% dark chocolate

Enchiladas are a favourite meal in our house. They're warm and filling, especially with this rich Mexican mole sauce. Don't be put off when you see chocolate in the list of ingredients – I'm not suggesting scattering chocolate chips on your dinner! Instead, a few squares of very dark chocolate melted into the sauce give it a delicious deep flavour and distinctive colour.

1. Put the oil into a non-stick pan on a medium heat. Add the bay leaf and cinnamon stick and warm them gently. Add the onion, celery and salt, and cook for a few minutes until it all gets soft and brown.

2. Add the red chilli, tomato purée, cumin, coriander and chilli powder and cook down for a few minutes. Throw in the tinned tomatoes and beans and cook gently for 15–20 minutes, until all the moisture has evaporated and the mixture is nice and dry.

3. Take off the heat, take out the bay leaf and cinnamon stick, and stir in the chopped coriander.

4. To make the mole sauce, put the oil, garlic, onion, salt, cumin, coriander, tomatoes, jalapeños and water into a pan and cook for about 10 minutes on a medium heat, until everything in the pan has softened. Take off the heat, stir in the chocolate and let it melt, then blend using either a stick blender or a regular blender.

5. Preheat the oven to 200°C/180°C fan/gas 6.

6. To assemble, put a little of the mole sauce into the base of a roasting dish or casserole dish.

7. Take a tortilla and place some of the black bean chilli in the centre, in a line. Fold over the shorter edges of the tortilla, then roll up and place in the dish. Repeat with the rest of the tortillas.

8. When all the enchiladas are in the dish, cover them with the rest of the mole sauce and sprinkle over the red onions and cheese. Bake in the oven for 25–30 minutes.

9. Remove from the oven and leave to stand for about 10 minutes before serving.

FISH PIE WITH CINNAMON SWEET POTATO

Serves 4

Fish pie is one of my favourite dishes to eat and to make. There's something comforting about food you can eat with just a fork: it's informal and leaves your other hand free to hold the hot plate underneath. Here, the fish is poached in coconut milk and topped with cinnamon sweet potato mash. It's also lactose-free, so I hope this recipe will appeal to everyone.

1. Put the olive oil, sweet potatoes, onion, cinnamon and salt into a medium pan and cook for 5 minutes. Add the water and place a lid on top. Cook for 12–15 minutes, until the potatoes are tender and all the water has evaporated. Mash the potatoes using the back of a fork, and set aside.

2. Preheat the oven to 200°C/180°C fan/gas 6.

3. Put the coconut milk into a medium pan with the bay leaves and bring to the boil. Add the fish and turn off the heat. Leave to poach in the residual heat for 5–10 minutes.

4. Meanwhile, put the eggs on to boil. They need about 9 minutes in a pan of boiling water.

5. Remove the fish to a plate, throw away the bay leaves and pour the hot coconut milk into a jug.

6. Add the oil to the empty pan and warm through. Now add the flour and mix well, stirring all the time. Pour the hot coconut milk back in and whisk until the mixture has thickened. Season to taste.

7. Add the sweetcorn and peas and mix. Add the fish and gently stir, making sure not to break up the pieces. Then pour the mixture into a 23cm round or square baking dish.

8. Carefully peel the hard-boiled eggs and cut each one into quarters. Dot the egg quarters across the fish mixture.

9. Roughly spoon the mashed sweet potato across the top of the pie and bake for 25–30 minutes.

PREP 40 MINUTES
COOK 25 MINUTES

For the cinnamon sweet potato

1 tablespoon olive oil

5 sweet potatoes (approx. 600g), peeled and cubed

1 medium onion (approx. 100g), roughly chopped

½ teaspoon ground cinnamon

salt, for seasoning

150ml water

For the fish pie

400ml coconut milk

5 bay leaves

340g fresh fish pie mix (cod, salmon, smoked pollock)

3 eggs

3 tablespoons olive oil

3 tablespoons plain flour

salt, for seasoning

70g tinned sweetcorn, drained

70g frozen peas, defrosted

INDIAN FIVE-SPICE VEGETABLE STIR-FRY

Serves 2

This is my go-to recipe on a weekly basis. I tend not to buy ready-mixed bags of stir-fry vegetables – although those are perfectly good for this recipe, I prefer to use up whatever I have left over in the fridge, since I always have stray veg left from other meals and I love nothing better than tarting them up in a hot wok with some of my favourite spices. Indian five-spice is a special blend of cumin, fenugreek, onion seeds, mustard and fennel seeds, which you can buy already mixed or you can mix yourself. The trick to a good stir-fry is to prepare all the vegetables beforehand and then it's just a matter of stirring and serving up.

PREP 30 MINUTES

COOK 10 MINUTES

2 spring onions, sliced diagonally

1 large red chilli, sliced diagonally (seeds in or out depending on how much heat you like)

1 carrot, thinly sliced into rounds

1 red pepper, thinly sliced

100g mangetout or sugar snaps

1 courgette, thinly sliced into matchsticks

150g tenderstem broccoli (or standard broccoli), florets thinly sliced

4 cloves of garlic, thinly sliced

6 tablespoons olive oil

salt and pepper, for seasoning

3 tablespoons sriracha sauce

15g fresh coriander

1 teaspoon Indian five-spice (blend of cumin, fenugreek, nigella seeds, mustard seeds and fennel seeds)

1. Prepare all the vegetables beforehand and this will seem like the easiest recipe you have ever cooked.

2. Put 2 tablespoons of the oil into a wok or a large non-stick frying pan. When the oil is really hot, add all the vegetables except the garlic, and begin cooking, making sure to stir and keep the vegetables moving. Season to taste.

3. Meanwhile, pour the remaining 4 tablespoons of oil into a small frying pan and heat on a medium heat. Add the garlic and fry till it is a very golden brown.

4. Add the sriracha and fresh coriander to the vegetables and mix through.

5. Add the five-spice to the garlic and heat just for a few seconds. Be careful not to burn the spices, they need to simply touch the hot oil to release their flavours. Pour all over the vegetables and stir through.

6. Serve the stir-fry immediately, while everything is still warm.

HERBY SKYR CHICKEN SALAD

Serves 2–4

Skyr is a cultured Icelandic yoghurt that has been around for thousands of years and is finally starting to make itself known in British supermarkets. It has the consistency of strained yoghurt but with a much milder taste. This is why it is so good with chicken, as it takes other flavours very well and really helps to get that meat lovely and tender. I have gone to town in this recipe and have added skyr to the dressing too.

1. To butterfly the chicken, lay each breast out flat. Using a sharp knife, cut into the breast down the centre. Make sure not to cut all the way through. Open each breast up like a book and flatten it, using the palm of your hand.

2. For the marinade, put the skyr, oil, parsley leaves, ground ginger, lemon juice and a couple of good grindings of salt and pepper into a food processor or a suitable container in which you can use a stick blender. Blend until smooth and green.

3. Put the butterflied chicken breasts in a freezer bag or container and add the marinade, mixing well to cover the chicken. Leave to marinate while you get on with the salad.

4. Boil the new potatoes for 15 minutes or until tender. Grate the courgette with the coarse side of a box grater. Using a veg peeler, shave the carrot into ribbons. Put the courgette and carrot into a serving bowl.

5. For the dressing, whisk together the skyr, olive oil, mustard, 1 teaspoon of vinegar and ½ teaspoon of honey, along with a pinch of salt and pepper. If the mixture is a little thick, add water a tablespoon at a time until the desired consistency is reached. You may only need one or two spoonfuls. Once combined, stir in the chopped chives. Taste and adjust the seasoning as necessary. Add a little more vinegar and/or honey if needed.

6. Halve the cooked potatoes and toss with a little of the dressing. Add to the bowl with the carrot and courgette.

7. To cook the chicken, heat a large, heavy-based frying pan over a medium high heat. Add a dash of oil and then the chicken breasts, opened out as flat as possible. Cook for 4 minutes, reducing the heat slightly if the chicken is darkening too quickly. Turn over and cook for a further 4 minutes.

8. Slice the chicken and place on top of the salad in the bowl. Drizzle over the rest of the dressing, garnish with more chopped chives and serve.

PREP 25 MINUTES
COOK 25 MINUTES

For the marinated chicken

2 chicken breasts

75g natural skyr

1 tablespoon olive oil, plus extra for cooking

a good handful of flat-leaf parsley leaves (about 20g)

1 teaspoon ground ginger

juice of ¼ of a lemon

salt and pepper

For the salad

250g new or baby potatoes

1 courgette

1 large carrot, peeled

For the dressing

50g natural skyr

25ml olive oil

1 teaspoon Dijon mustard

1–1½ teaspoons cider vinegar

½ –1 teaspoon runny honey

salt and pepper

4 tablespoons finely chopped fresh chives, plus extra for garnish

MEATBALL SLIDER SUBS

Serves 4

My 21-year-old brother often sees something he wants to eat on his travels (and by travels, I mean the distance between uni and the gym, not to mention his journeys on YouTube) and texts me a picture asking, 'Can you make this?' Anyone who knows me (and he knows me very well) also knows that I like a challenge. So this recipe is one of those things he spotted in a sandwich shop window and challenged me to do better. Soft sub roll, fragrant meatballs, rich tomato sauce, melted mozzarella. Simple but delicious. Challenge won, and my brother agrees.

PREP 30 MINUTES
COOK 45 MINUTES

For the meatballs

900g lamb mince

1 teaspoon salt

2 teaspoons chipotle chilli flakes (see tip, opposite)

2 teaspoons garam masala

5 tablespoons crispy onions (pots sold in supermarkets)

4 soft sub rolls, to serve

For the sauce

3 tablespoons olive oil

3 cloves of garlic, finely diced

1 medium onion, chopped

1 teaspoon salt

100ml cold water

350g passata

2 teaspoons mango powder (see tip, opposite)

2 teaspoons chipotle chilli flakes (see tip, opposite)

1 teaspoon garam masala

15g fresh coriander, roughly chopped

2 mozzarella balls, drained and sliced

5 teaspoons crispy onions

1. Put the mince into a large bowl along with the salt, chilli flakes, garam masala and crispy onions. Get your hands in and give it all a good mix.

2. Wet your hands a little with water or grease them with oil. This will stop the mince sticking to your hands while shaping.

3. Shape the mince mix into 12 equal balls, making sure to pack it tightly in your hands. Set aside on a plate, covered, in the fridge while you get started on the sauce.

4. Put the oil into a large non-stick frying pan (big enough to cook all the meatballs at once) and place on a medium heat.

5. Add the garlic, onion and salt, and cook till the onion is soft and translucent.

6. Add the water and cook until the onion is very soft and the water has evaporated.

7. Now add the passata, along with mango powder, chilli flakes, garam masala and coriander, and cook for 10 minutes on a medium heat.

8. Add the meatballs to the pan. Don't be tempted to stir or they will break up. Place a lid on the pan and leave the meatballs to steam on a low to medium heat for about 10 minutes.

9. Take off the lid and you will see that the meatballs look pale on top and will have firmed up, so there is no longer a risk of them breaking. Give them a stir – they may have stuck slightly on the base, but that will all add to the flavour. Make sure the balls are covered with the sauce. Put the lid back on and cook for another 15 minutes on a low to medium heat.

10. Meanwhile, turn the oven on to 200°C/180°C/gas 6.

11. Split the subs along the edge, making sure to keep one half attached. Place on a baking tray and toast in the oven for 5 minutes.

12. Take out and fill the subs with three meatballs each.

13. Using half a mozzarella ball per sub, place some sliced mozzarella on top of each meatball and put back into the oven for another 6–7 minutes, or until the mozzarella is melting.

14. Take out of the oven and, just before serving, drizzle some of the leftover sauce into the sub and sprinkle the fried onions on top. Serve while still warm.

Tips: If you can't find chipotle chilli flakes, use regular chilli flakes or mix 2 teaspoons of regular chilli flakes with ½ teaspoon of smoked paprika for the smoky flavour.

Mango powder can be found in most Asian supermarkets, or you can substitute the juice of ½ a lemon, or 1 tablespoon of tamarind paste.

BAY-INFUSED COQ AU 'VIN' WITH CREAMY MASH

Serves 6

Just because I don't drink alcohol, I don't see why it should deter me as a cook. Rather than let it put me off my cooking adventures, I almost always find a substitute. So when I came across this classic French dish I had to give it a go. The appeal was the beautiful deeply coloured chicken, and by substituting the wine with grape juice I still get a vibrant colour and also a gorgeous sweetness. So never be deterred – there's always another way if you look for it!

**PREP 25 MINUTES,
PLUS MARINATING
COOK 1 HOUR 20 MINUTES**

For the coq au vin

12 skinless chicken thighs
(approx. 1kg)

700ml red grape juice

5 bay leaves

50g unsalted butter

5 cloves of garlic, crushed

1 small onion (approx. 150g),
finely chopped

1 teaspoon salt

350g button mushrooms

500ml chicken stock

2 tablespoons Worcestershire
sauce

leaves from 4 sprigs of thyme

1½ tablespoons cornflour

For the mash

1.5kg potatoes, peeled and cut
into chunks

125ml double cream

2 tablespoons unsalted butter

5 tablespoons full-fat
mayonnaise

½ teaspoon salt

1. Soak the chicken thighs in the grape juice with the bay leaves overnight for maximum colour. If you are short of time, you can do this stage a few hours ahead.

2. Take the thigh pieces out and dry them with kitchen paper. Leave the grape juice and bay leaves to one side for later.

3. Place a large casserole dish on a medium to high heat and add the butter. Once the butter has melted, add the chicken pieces and brown them on both sides. Take the chicken out and set aside.

4. Add the garlic, onion and salt to the pan and cook for a few minutes, until the onion has softened.

5. Now add the mushrooms, chicken stock, Worcestershire sauce, thyme and the grape juice and bay leaves you set aside earlier.

6. Let everything come to the boil, then put the chicken back in, add the lid and cook for 50 minutes to 1 hour on a medium heat.

7. Meanwhile, make the mash. Boil the potatoes in cold water until they are tender – this should take about 15 minutes. Drain, then put them back into the pan to dry out any extra moisture.

8. Mash the potatoes using a masher or a potato ricer. I love using a ricer because it really does get rid of every single lump. A worthwhile investment.

9. Heat the cream and butter in a pan, until the cream comes to a quick boil. Add to the mashed potatoes. Mix in the mayonnaise and seasoning.

10. Once the chicken is cooked, put the cornflour into a small bowl with 3 tablespoons of cold water and mix well. Stir into the pan of chicken and mushrooms, then cook, covered, on a low heat for 3-4 minutes to thicken the sauce.

11. Serve the coq au 'vin' with the mashed potato.

YORKSHIRE PUDDINGS
SWEET & SAVOURY
—— *Makes 4 savoury and 12 sweet* ——

This recipe gives an insight into how my cooking brain works. Having lived in Yorkshire, married a Yorkshireman and given birth to three Yorkshire babies, I just can't get away from all things Yorkshire. In our house, we like to use Yorkshire puddings as bowls and fill them with beef and horseradish and some crisp cooked broccoli or seasonal veg. While I'm about it, I make twelve extra small Yorkshires and fill them with spoonfuls of canned custard and strawberry jam, for afters! The jam in this recipe requires no boiling, just a tiny bit of patience to let the magic of the dried basil seeds happen. If you can't find dried basil seeds, chia seeds also work.) So let me introduce you to my showstopper Yorkshire puddings, dinner and dessert style.

PREP 50 MINUTES,
PLUS CHILLING
COOK 2 HOURS

For the Yorkshire puddings
140g plain flour, sifted

4 large eggs

200ml whole milk

a pinch of salt

about 120ml sunflower oil

For the sweet puds
150g strawberries, hulled
and halved

4 teaspoon dried basil seeds
or chia seeds

1 x 400g tin of
ready-made custard

fresh strawberries, to
garnish (optional)

squirty cream, to garnish
(optional)

1. The Yorkshire pudding batter and the jam both benefit from being made early and left overnight. You can also make the beef and horseradish a day in advance if you want, and then reheat it when you need it (but don't stir the parsley through until just before serving).

2. For the batter, place the sifted flour in a large mixing bowl, add the eggs and mix to a stiff batter. Now pour in the milk slowly, whisking all the time until it has been incorporated and the mixture is free of any lumps. Season, stir, then transfer the mixture to a large jug, cover with cling film and leave in the fridge overnight. Allowing the batter to chill lets any air bubbles settle, and when the cold batter eventually comes into contact with the hot oil this helps produce a fast rise.

3. Now for the jam. Blitz the strawberries in a blender or with a hand-held blender to get a smooth paste. Add the dried basil or chia seeds and mix well. You will see the mixture instantly begin to thicken and take on a jam-like texture. Transfer to a small bowl, cover and put into the fridge to chill.

4. The following day (or you can also do it in advance if you want), make the beef and horseradish. Put the beef into a bowl and season. Add the flour and mix so all the beef is coated. Put 1 tablespoon of the oil into a large non-stick pan on a medium to high heat and brown the beef in three batches, being sure not to overcrowd the pan. You're not cooking the beef, you're just getting a golden colour and crust on the meat. Set aside.

5. Add another glug of oil to the pan. Add the garlic, onion, salt, nutmeg and yeast extract, and cook gently till the onions are browned and really soft. Add the potatoes and mushrooms and cook for another 5 minutes, just to get a bit of colour on the vegetables.

6. Return the meat to the pan. Add the stock and bring the whole thing to a rapid boil, then reduce the heat, cover and simmer until the mixture has thickened and the meat is tender (about 1 hour 15 minutes). If the sauce is thin, lift out the meat and veg, bubble the sauce until thickened and reduced, then stir the meat and vegetables back in. Add the horseradish and chopped parsley right at the end and mix it through.

7. Now it's time to cook the Yorkshires. Preheat the oven to 230°C/210° fan/gas 8. Have two baking trays ready, a four-hole Yorkshire pudding tray for the large ones and a twelve-hole bun tin for the small ones. Pour sunflower oil into the base of each cavity, about 2–3 teaspoons in each large hole and 1 teaspoon in each small one, so the bases are fully covered.

8. Put the trays into the oven for about 10 minutes, until the oil is really hot and begins to smoke a little.

9. Take the batter out of the fridge (and also take out the jam at this point, so it has time to come up to room temperature). Take the trays out of the oven, pour the batter straight on top of the oil, to come about two-thirds of the way up the holes, and immediately put back into the oven. Don't get distracted at this point, as timing is absolutely key to a successful Yorkshire pudding. The small Yorkshires will need about 15 minutes and the large ones need about 20 minutes. Be sure not to open the oven until you're ready to get the small ones out. Once baked, set aside, leaving them in the tray.

10. Meanwhile, put the broccoli florets into a microwaveable dish, add 2 tablespoons of water and cover with cling film. Microwave for 5 minutes on high – this will lightly steam the broccoli without overcooking. Take off the cling film and season with a little salt and pepper.

11. Divide the beef between the four large Yorkshires, along with the broccoli, and serve warm.

12. Leave the twelve small Yorkshires to cool completely. After you have finished your main course, top the mini Yorkshires with spoonfuls of custard and strawberry jam. I like to serve them with fresh strawberries and squirty cream.

For the beef puds

450g braising steak or skirt, cut into 2½cm pieces

salt and pepper, for seasoning

2 tablespoons plain flour

4 tablespoons olive oil

3 cloves of garlic, crushed and chopped

1 medium onion, chopped

1 teaspoon salt

½ teaspoon ground nutmeg

1 teaspoon yeast extract

10 baby potatoes, halved (about 300g)

250g chestnut mushrooms, whole

500ml beef stock

3 tablespoons horseradish

15g fresh flat-leaf parsley, roughly chopped

1 large head of broccoli, broken into florets

Friends Over

There's nothing like a meal together for saying thank you, I've missed you, or I just want to see your face. Between working and looking after the children and the house, I don't often get lots of time to cook or entertain. Luckily my work involves a lot of recipe testing and recipe tasting, so nobody at home ever really misses out on eating by the truckload. We eat all day, every day! But cooking with purpose has a very different feel to it. Especially if it's cooking with purpose and people in mind. I have the ability to turn a meeting at home into a three-course dinner party. These are some of my favourite recipes to feed a crowd of family or friends, or both. My crowds often involve more children than adults, so these recipes please everyone around the table.

CARAMELIZED ONION SOUP WITH CAYENNE CROUTONS

Serves 4

Soups don't always have to come out of a tin (not that there is anything wrong with that), and they sure don't need to be tricky. Taking a simple ingredient like onion and enhancing it by cooking it gently is enough to create a stunning rich soup that's almost as easy as opening a can. Not as easy, but almost as easy. And delicious topped with these cayenne croutons.

1. Put a large pan on a medium heat and add the butter. Once it's hot, add the crushed garlic and sliced onions. Cook for about 15–20 minutes, until the onions have softened significantly and reduced down completely.

2. Add the salt and sugar and 100ml of the stock and allow it all to cook for another 10 minutes. The onions should be a nice golden brown.

3. Now add the cornflour mixture, along with the rest of the stock. Bring to the boil, then leave to simmer gently for 30 minutes.

4. Meanwhile preheat the oven to 190°C/170°C fan/gas 5.

5. Lay the bread on a baking tray. Mix the cayenne and salt with the oil. Brush both sides of the bread with the oil/cayenne mix and toast in the oven for 20 minutes, making sure to turn the slices halfway. Bake until the bread is very crisp and dry.

6. Once the onion soup is ready, set aside for 10 minutes and then, using a stick blender, blitz it until it's smooth.

7. Pour into individual bowls, sprinkle with the thyme leaves and break shards of the cayenne croutons on top.

PREP 30 MINUTES
COOK 1 HOUR

For the onion soup

100g unsalted butter

3 cloves of garlic, crushed

3 medium onions (approx. 450g), thinly sliced

¼ teaspoon salt

2 teaspoons light brown sugar

1 litre vegetable stock

2 tablespoons cornflour (mixed with 4 tablespoons cold water)

6 sprigs of lemon thyme, leaves picked

For the croutons

2 slices of white bread

½–1 teaspoon cayenne pepper, depending on how hot you like it

¼ teaspoon fine salt

4 tablespoons olive oil

CARROT, CUMIN & CORIANDER SOUP

Serves 4

Making soup wasn't something that I used to venture into much. I was happy warming up tinned tomato soup in my milk pan and eating it with crusty bread. Until one day I decided to go off-piste and buy a fancy gourmet carrot and coriander soup, and, without revealing the brand, it was utterly horrific. I tried to suppress my annoyance by making my own, much tastier version. Don't get me wrong, I still love tomato soup out of a tin, but I like making this recipe from scratch.

PREP 20 MINUTES
COOK 50 MINUTES

1 tablespoon coriander seeds

1 tablespoon cumin seeds

2 tablespoons olive oil

1 onion (approx. 150g),
chopped
½ teaspoon salt

450g carrots,
skins kept on, grated

1 potato (approx. 150g),
peeled and grated

1 litre vegetable stock

a large handful of
fresh coriander (approx. 30g),
chopped

1. Find a large pan for the soup. Place it on a medium heat and add the coriander and cumin seeds. Stir the seeds and wait to hear some popping. As soon as you hear it, add the oil to the pan.

2. Now add the onion and salt and cook gently for 5 minutes.

3. Add the carrots and potato and cook for 10 minutes on a medium to high heat.

4. Add the stock and allow the whole lot to simmer for 30 minutes, until the carrots are soft.

5. Using a stick blender, blitz to a smooth soup.

6. Stir in the fresh coriander and serve.

RICE GINGER FEETA WITH SWEET MANGO PICKLE

Serves 4 (makes 16)

These are classic Bangladeshi fritters that are eaten with a cup of tea. They are made of steamed ginger and rice flour, and fried for a crisp exterior and soft inside. I also love them as a starter. They are simple, quick to make, and freeze well for whenever you need something in a hurry. They work well on their own but taste even better with a sweet mango pickle.

1. Put the water into a pan with the salt, ginger and turmeric. Bring to the boil over a high heat, then turn down to a gentle simmer. Mix in the rice flour.

2. Turn the heat off and keep mixing to get rid of as many lumps as possible.

3. Put the lid on the pan and leave to steam for 30 minutes, still with the heat turned off.

4. Dust your work surface with rice flour, then take the dough out of the pan and leave on the work surface for 15 minutes to cool before handling.

5. Dust your hands with rice flour and knead the dough to a smooth consistency. It will be quite sticky at first, so be sure to use plenty of flour.

6. Roll the dough out on a floured surface to about ½cm thick, then, using a floured 5cm cutter, cut out rounds. Roll out the offcuts and repeat until all the dough has been used up.

7. Heat the oil in a large deep pan. When it's hot (180°C, if you happen to have a cooking thermometer), put in a few of the dough pieces at a time, making sure not to overcrowd the pan. Fry them for 3–4 minutes.

8. Drain on kitchen paper, then fry the rest in batches.

9. Serve with sweet mango pickle.

PREP 20 MINUTES
COOK 50 MINUTES

400ml water

1 teaspoon salt

100g fresh ginger, peeled and crushed

1 teaspoon ground turmeric

200g rice flour, plus extra for dusting

1.5 litres oil, for frying

sweet mango pickle, to serve

CRAB CAKES WITH LEMON MAYO

Serves 8 (makes 24)

I love creating little bites to eat. It's a perfect way of sharing and enjoying food together. When I first started to cook with crab, and quite excitedly declared this to my grandmother, she was most appalled. She said, 'We only eat fish, meat and chicken and that's it. Why would you eat a crab?' So it's safe to say she wouldn't try my crab cakes, but everyone else did. If you're not a fan of crab, you can make these substituting the same amount of fish for the crab. But personally, I love the sweetness of the crab paired with this lemon mayo dip.

**PREP 20 MINUTES,
PLUS CHILLING
COOK 20 MINUTES**

For the crab cakes

20g fresh ginger, peeled and crushed, either shop-bought or use a pestle and mortar

1 small red onion (approx. 100g), finely chopped

a large handful of fresh coriander (approx. 30g), chopped

1 small red chilli, finely chopped (deseed if you want it less spicy)

1 teaspoon salt

250g mashed potato, cooled (see tip below)

850g tinned or fresh crabmeat (mix of brown and white), excess moisture squeezed out

1 large egg, lightly beaten

100g plain flour, for dusting

about 50ml olive oil, for frying

For the lemon mayo dip

6 tablespoons (about 90g) mayonnaise

zest and juice of 1 lemon

salt and pepper, for seasoning

1. Put the crushed ginger, chopped onion, coriander, chilli, salt, mashed potato, crabmeat and egg into a large bowl. Get your hands in and give it a good mix, making sure it is all incorporated really well.

2. Divide the mixture into 24 equal balls, then wet your hands and shape into flat round patties.

3. Dust each crab cake with a light coating of flour. Place on a tray and leave to chill in the fridge for 15 minutes.

4. Put some oil into a pan on a medium heat and add the crab cakes, making sure not to overcrowd the pan. Fry them in batches, making sure to wipe out the oil and any burnt bits in the pan and adding fresh oil each time.

5. Fry the crab cakes for approximately 3 minutes on each side, or until they are golden brown on both sides.

6. For the lemon mayo dip, put the mayo, lemon zest and juice, salt and pepper into a bowl and mix.

Tip: To make 250g of mash from scratch, cook 1 large (300g) potato in the microwave for 10–15 minutes in 5-minute bursts, then peel and mash the flesh.

AUBERGINE PAKORAS WITH SPICED KETCHUP

Serves 4 (makes 18–20)

These are a firm favourite during the month of Ramadan, when we fast from the point of the sun rising until it sets in the evening. That can last up to 18 hours. By which point, your heart desires nothing but fried food, creamy desserts and mountains of carbs. These pakoras are a favourite of my dad and sister, and we make them especially for them. The batter can be used to coat an array of vegetables: aubergine is my favourite, but you can dabble with potatoes, okra, cauliflower and even kale.

PREP 25 MINUTES
COOK 15–20 MINUTES

For the pakoras

125g chickpea flour

1 teaspoon salt

1 teaspoon baking powder

1 teaspoon ground coriander

1 teaspoon paprika

1 teaspoon garlic powder

1 teaspoon ground cumin

140ml water

1.5 litres vegetable oil,
for frying

2 aubergines (each approx.
300g), cut lengthways into
½cm thick slices

For the spiced ketchup

5 tablespoons (approx. 75g)
tomato ketchup

5 tablespoons (75ml) water

1 fresh green chilli

a pinch of salt

2 tablespoons chopped
fresh coriander

½ red onion (approx. 50g),
finely chopped

1. Put the chickpea flour, salt, baking powder, coriander, paprika, garlic powder and cumin into a bowl and mix with a whisk. Add the water and mix to a smooth paste.

2. Heat the oil to 150°C, if you have a thermometer. If not, drop in a small bit of batter – if it sizzles and rises to the top, the oil is ready to start frying with.

3. Dip slices of aubergine into the batter and cover completely, then drop into the oil. Fry in batches for 3-4 minutes, or until they are golden brown, then put them on a baking tray lined with kitchen paper to mop up any oil.

4. To make the sauce, put the ketchup, water, chilli, salt and coriander into a food processor and blitz to a smooth paste. Transfer to a small serving bowl and mix in the chopped onion. Serve with the pakoras, for dipping.

Photo overleaf →

CURRY, CARROT & PARSNIP BHAJIS WITH CORIANDER & CHILLI CHUTNEY

Serves 4 (makes 20)

I am an over-zealous carrot buyer. I buy far more than I need. Week in, week out, I never learn. Because I am always left with too many carrots, it always results in an end-of-week carrot cake, which may sound like a good thing but, what with all the other cakes and desserts flying about in our house, isn't always welcome! So I've devised a few recipes for using up my root veg at the end of the week in ways that aren't carrot cakes. Here I fry my carrots instead.

1. Put the carrots, parsnips, chickpea flour, cumin, curry powder, coriander and salt into a large bowl and mix with your hands to release some of the moisture from the carrots and parsnips.

2. Add the eggs and mix in well. The mixture should be like a thick batter. Almost like an uncooked carrot cake batter.

3. Heat the oil to 150°C, if you have a thermometer. If you don't, you will know the oil is ready if you drop in a little batter and it sizzles and comes to the top.

4. Working in batches, drop heaped teaspoons of the batter into the oil and cook for 3–4 minutes, making sure to turn the bhajis all the time so they are an even golden colour.

5. Drain on kitchen paper while you cook the rest.

6. To make the chutney, put the coriander, chillies, lemon juice, oil, salt and sugar into a food processor and blitz to a smooth paste. Serve with the bhajis.

Tip: These can be cooled, placed in a ziplock bag and frozen. Reheat in a warm oven.

Photo overleaf →

PREP 30 MINUTES
COOK 20 MINUTES

For the bhajis

150g carrots, grated

150g parsnips, grated

120g chickpea flour

1 teaspoon ground cumin

1 teaspoon curry powder

1 teaspoon ground coriander

1 teaspoon salt

2 medium eggs

1.5–2 litres vegetable oil, for frying

For the chutney

a large handful of fresh coriander (approx. 50g)

3 fresh green chillies

3 tablespoons lemon juice

1 teaspoon olive oil

½ teaspoon salt

1 teaspoon caster sugar

GOAT'S CHEESE &
RED PEPPER GALETTES

Serves 4

A galette is like an open pie, a tart or a pizza – whichever you like. Much as I love the surprise of seeing the inside of a pie when it is cut or spooned, I also like seeing the beautiful fillings displayed in all their glory. In these individual galettes, the vibrant and sweet cooked red peppers work well with the salty goat's cheese. (I still can't convince my children that goat's cheese doesn't taste of goat, nor can I convince my husband either. Well, never mind, all four for me, in that case!)

1. Put the flour into a bowl. Add the yeast on one side of the bowl and the salt on the other. Add the sugar and give it all a quick mix.

2. Make a well in the centre and add the oil and water. Using a palette knife, bring the liquids together with the dry ingredients.

3. The mixture will be quite wet, so dust the work surface with flour and knead the dough for 5 minutes until the dough is smooth. Put it back into the bowl, cover with cling film, and leave on the worktop.

4. Meanwhile, put the oil and garlic into a pan on a medium heat. Cook the garlic for a minute, then add the onions and salt. Cook until the onions are totally soft, which can take about 10 minutes.

5. Now add the peppers and passata and cook for another 15–20 minutes, until the peppers have softened completely. Set aside and leave to cool.

6. Preheat the oven to 220°C/220°C fan/gas 7 and line 2 baking trays with baking paper.

7. Take the dough out of the bowl. Knead for a minute, then cut it into four equal pieces. On a floured surface, roll out each piece of dough as thinly as possible, to a 23cm circle. Place the circles of dough on the prepared trays.

8. Spread the red pepper mix over each circle, making sure to leave 5cm of the pastry exposed around the edge. Dot the goat's cheese all over.

9. Lift the edges of the pastry and fold over, not in a neat fashion, just roughly. Brush with the melted garlic butter and bake in the oven for 12–14 minutes.

10. Once baked, drizzle the galettes with olive oil and garnish the top with rocket leaves.

PREP 40 MINUTES,
PLUS RESTING
COOK 45 MINUTES

For the base

300g strong bread flour,
plus extra for dusting

7g fast-action yeast

1 teaspoon salt

1 teaspoon caster sugar

3 tablespoons olive oil

200ml warm water

For the filling

3 tablespoons olive oil

2 cloves of garlic, crushed

1 small onion (approx. 100g),
chopped

½ teaspoon salt

2 large red peppers
(approx. 400g), thinly sliced

300ml passata

250g goat's cheese,
cut into chunks

20g garlic butter, melted
(or normal salted butter)

rocket leaves and olive oil,
for dressing

CHEESE SCONES WITH CHIVE BUTTER

Serves 6

However you like to pronounce them, scones were one of the first things that I ever baked. I think they are still a staple in teaching kids how to bake, as my nephew came home with these beauties a few years ago when he started to cook at school. I have made so many variations on the classic and there is a good reason for that: they are simple, easy and so versatile. These cheese ones are perfect to start or end a meal with. See, I told you they were versatile. Now all I have to do is find a way of making them acceptable to keep in my gym bag.

PREP 30 MINUTES
COOK 15 MINUTES

For the scones

175g self-raising flour

50g strong white flour, plus extra for dusting

¼ teaspoon onion salt

55g unsalted butter

25g red Leicester cheese, grated

150ml whole milk, plus 2–3 tablespoons milk, for glazing

For the chive butter

80g unsalted butter, softened

1 teaspoon rock salt

20g fresh chives, finely chopped

1. Preheat the oven to 220°C/200°C fan/gas 7. Line a baking tray with baking paper.

2. Put the flours, onion salt and butter into a large bowl. Rub the butter in with your fingertips until it has mixed in well and created a breadcrumb texture.

3. Add the cheese and mix through. Make a well in the centre and add the milk. Mix with a palette knife, then use your hands to bring the dough together. Be careful not to knead, or the dough will become tough.

4. Dust your worktop with flour and push the dough out to a thickness of about 2cm.

5. Using a 5cm cutter, using one downward motion, cut out the scones and lay them on the tray. Bring the offcuts together, being careful not to knead. Cut out as many circles as you can until you run out of dough.

6. Brush the tops with milk and bake for 12–15 minutes, until the scones are golden and well risen.

7. To make the chive butter, mix the softened butter with the salt and chives. Lay out a piece of cling film and tip out the butter on to it. Tease the cling film so the butter makes a sausage shape. Wrap and twist the ends, then refrigerate and serve in slices with the scones.

APPLE, WALNUT & CORIANDER SALAD WITH BURNT GARLIC DRESSING

Serves 4

I love a simple salad to start a meal, so I can nosedive straight into dinner and then dessert. It's a lovely way of balancing a meal. I also think it's nice to have a salad that doesn't scream out diet or healthy eating. In this one, the tart apple complements the crunch of the nuts and the aroma of the burnt garlic dressing. It's a sophisticated yet not very complicated salad that will get your mates thinking you've tried really hard.

1. Prepare the apple, sprinkle the lemon juice on top and stir the juice in. This will stop the apple going brown.

2. Put the rocket and coriander leaves into a large bowl. Add the apples and walnuts and toss through.

3. To prepare the dressing, burn the garlic by placing it on the edge of a small gas hob and turning the flame on low so it can catch the edges and turn the garlic completely black. Alternatively, use a blowtorch and burn the garlic completely.

4. Keeping the charred skins on, chop the garlic as fine as you can possibly get it. Then, using the back of a knife, crush the chopped garlic to release the flavour. Put it into a jar with a lid, then add the salt, oil, vinegar and mayonnaise. Put the lid on and give it a good shake.

5. Dress your salad with as much or as little dressing as you like. Whatever is left over can be kept in the fridge for another salad.

PREP 15 MINUTES
COOK 5 MINUTES

For the salad

2 Granny Smith apples, cored, quartered and thinly sliced

2 tablespoons lemon juice

90g rocket leaves

a large handful of fresh coriander leaves (approx. 25g)

100g toasted walnuts, roughly chopped

For the dressing

3 cloves of garlic, not peeled

a large pinch of salt

150ml olive oil

50ml balsamic vinegar

1 tablespoon mayonnaise

TOFU COCONUT KATSU CURRY

Serves 4

Tofu comes in so many different varieties. As I travel, as I read, as I learn about new cuisines, I see how versatile this wonderful ingredient can be. It is a great bearer of flavour and is beautiful stewed, fried, smoked or cooked. It is a thing of beauty. I never tell anyone beforehand when I'm cooking them tofu because I don't like the preconceived notion that it isn't delicious. I love their reaction when they taste it and then I tell them that it's tofu.

PREP 30 MINUTES
COOK 1 HOUR 10 MINUTES

For the sauce

1 tablespoon olive oil

5 cloves of garlic, crushed

1 onion (approx. 100g), chopped

1 teaspoon salt

2 tablespoons brown sugar (light or dark)

2 carrots (approx. 200g), peeled and chopped

1 tablespoon curry powder

1 tablespoon garam masala

2 tablespoons desiccated coconut

2 tablespoons plain flour

600ml vegetable stock, hot

3 spring onions, sliced thinly

For the rice

375g basmati rice

830ml water

For the tofu

4 pieces (100g each) of tofu

salt, for seasoning

1 large egg, beaten

50g panko breadcrumbs

5 tablespoons olive oil

1. Place a big pan on a medium heat and add the oil. Add the garlic, onion, salt and brown sugar and cook for 5 minutes, until the onions are soft.

2. Add the carrots, curry powder, garam masala and desiccated coconut and cook for 10 minutes. Add the flour and stir in for a minute.

3. Now add the hot stock and simmer for 30 minutes, until the carrots are soft.

4. Using a stick blender, blitz the sauce, then strain it through a sieve to remove any lumps. Put back in the pan and leave on a very low heat.

5. Put the rice into a medium pan with the water and bring to the boil, stirring occasionally. This takes about 5 minutes.

6. Once all the water has evaporated (about 5–10 minutes), turn the heat down, put the lid on and let the rice steam. It needs about another 10 minutes.

7. Season the tofu and dip it first into the beaten egg and then into the breadcrumbs.

8. Place a non-stick pan on a medium heat and add the oil. Fry the tofu for 3 minutes on each side, until golden and crisp.

9. Serve the rice topped with slices of crisp tofu. Pour over the hot katsu sauce, and sprinkle with the spring onions.

Tip: This recipe makes a generous amount of sauce (about 800ml). Any leftovers will keep in the fridge for a couple of days, or can be frozen for up to a month.

CHICKEN & CHORIZO PAELLA

Serves 4

I love any dish that involves maximum flavour and minimum washing up. This is one of those dishes. Even better, you can change it around quite simply with the protein of your choice. I enjoy this combination of spicy chorizo and chicken with the slowly cooked rice.

1. Heat a large flat pan to a medium heat. Add 2 tablespoons of oil and, once it's hot, add the diced chorizo and chicken thighs. Cook for 10 minutes, until all the chicken is cooked through.

2. Using a slotted spoon, remove the chorizo and chicken from the pan and keep the pan on the heat. Add the rest of the oil, along with the garlic, onions and salt, and cook for 10 minutes, until the onions are soft. Now add the rice and cook over a high heat for 2 minutes, making sure to scrape the bottom, as all of that contains flavour.

3. Add the smoked paprika and chopped tomatoes and cook for a further 10 minutes, until the tomatoes have softened.

4. Add all the stock and cook on a high heat with the lid off, stirring occasionally. Once the moisture has almost completely evaporated (this takes about 12 minutes), add the chicken and chorizo and stir through. Cook for 10 minutes on a low heat.

5. Sprinkle over the parsley and add the lemon wedges to serve.

PREP 20 MINUTES
COOK 45 MINUTES

5 tablespoons olive oil

200g chorizo, cubed

200g skinless boneless chicken thighs, diced

2 cloves of garlic, crushed

1 large onion (approx. 200g), chopped

1 teaspoon salt

300g paella rice

1 teaspoon smoked paprika

4 tomatoes (approx. 400g), chopped

900ml chicken stock, hot

a large handful of fresh parsley (30g), chopped

1 lemon, cut into wedges

JERK HADDOCK & JOLLOF RICE SALAD

Serves 4

The first time I ate Caribbean food was a lucky accident. I found myself out and about with kids that needed feeding. They would have eaten the leather off their shoes if I hadn't found something fast. I was run ragged, lugging three enormous bags and three moody children in the rain, so when I spotted a little Caribbean café on the corner, there was no hesitating, though the smells alone would have been enough to entice me in. We ordered far more food than planned and came back out with very happy stomachs! We then visited that cafe every week for a long time afterwards, hungry for more. I have tried using the same flavours in my kitchen and have found many variations that work, such as this delicious fish.

PREP 30 MINUTES

COOK 25 MINUTES

For the jerk haddock

2 tablespoons each of ground cinnamon, ground black pepper, dried thyme, ground allspice and paprika

1 teaspoon grated nutmeg

1 teaspoon salt

2 tablespoons plain flour

4 x 200g haddock fillets

5 tablespoons olive oil

For the jollof rice

125g each of cold cooked white rice and black rice (from precooked pouches)

1 red onion, chopped

1 large red pepper, diced

2 large tomatoes (approx. 200g), deseeded and chopped

10g fresh ginger, peeled and finely chopped

2 thin slices of Scotch bonnet chilli, finely chopped

2 tablespoons olive oil

salt, for seasoning

1. Preheat the oven to 180°C/160°C fan/gas 4.

2. Mix all the dried spices and salt in a bowl, stir in the flour, and transfer to a jar.

3. Put the haddock fillets on a large baking tray and sprinkle over 3 tablespoons of the jerk seasoning. Put the remainder away for another day.

4. Pour the oil over the fish, then rub in the oil and spices.

5. Place in the oven and bake for 20–25 minutes.

6. To make the jollof salad, put the black and white rice into a bowl. Add the onion, pepper, tomatoes, ginger, Scotch bonnet and olive oil, season to taste and mix well.

7. Serve the fish with the salad alongside.

WHOLE BAKED FISH WITH POTATOES, LEMON & SUN-DRIED TOMATOES

Serves 4

I grew up eating a lot of fish, as it's a staple of any Bangladeshi home. My mother would use all kinds of exotic fish that were cooked and preserved in various complicated ways before even making it into the stewing pot. But my travels round Britain have shown me fish in a different light, and I've discovered much simpler and far quicker ways of cooking it. It's given me a whole new appreciation of its sweet and subtle flavours. This recipe looks and sounds impressive, but is actually very straightforward, with the whole fish baked gently on a bed of potatoes and sun-dried tomatoes. The addition of sliced lemons and sugar adds loads of delicious flavour to the flesh and juices.

PREP 15 MINUTES
COOK 40 MINUTES

750g new potatoes

1 small unwaxed lemon, sliced

1 tablespoon black
onion seeds

1 x 280g jar of sun-dried
tomatoes in oil

salt and pepper, for seasoning

2 teaspoons caster sugar

2 x 400–500g whole fish,
such as sea bass, sea trout or
Dover sole, scaled and gutted.

a small bunch of fresh parsley

a small bunch of fresh
lemon thyme

1. Preheat the oven to 200°C/180°C fan/gas 6 and line a large baking dish or roasting tin with baking paper.

2. Boil the potatoes in salted water for 10 minutes or until just becoming tender. Drain, then slice them lengthways into about ½cm thick slices. Place them in the lined dish or tin and mix in the sliced lemon and the onion seeds.

3. Remove the sun-dried tomatoes from their oil, reserving the oil, and roughly chop. Mix the tomatoes into the potatoes, along with 3 tablespoons of the reserved oil. Season with salt and pepper and mix in the sugar.

4. Season the fish inside and out and place half the herbs inside each one. (If using Dover sole, lay the herbs between the fish and the potatoes.) Place the fish on top of the potatoes and drizzle over a couple of tablespoons of the remaining sun-dried tomato oil.

5. Bake for 25–30 minutes, or until the fish is just cooked through and the potatoes are crisping up. Remove from the oven, and serve.

GOAT TAGINE WITH ORZO & DATES

Serves 4

Where food is concerned, I'm not a massive follower of rules, and I love nothing more than recipes where different worlds collide, especially if they can be cooked in one pot. Here the flavours of a Moroccan tagine are filled out with Italian orzo, while the star of the show is goat, a meat not eaten often enough in my opinion, but one which is gradually becoming more common in Britain. Goat was always my grandfather's meat of choice, so this is for him. I don't know what he would have thought of my recipe, but I do know he would have been proud to see me using goat meat. Its flavour works well with sweet dates, while the orzo and crisp pitta make this a really hearty meal.

1. Make slits in the base and tops of the tomatoes, place them in a bowl, fill with boiling water and cover with cling film.

2. Put 1 tablespoon of oil into a large non-stick pan and place on a medium heat. Add the goat chunks in three batches and cook the meat until it's browned all over, then remove from the pan and set aside.

3. Add another tablespoon of oil if the pan is dry, then add the garlic, onion and salt and cook for a few minutes, till the onions have softened. Add the cinnamon, ginger and paprika, and cook gently, keeping the heat low so the spices don't burn. Put the goat back into the pan and stir to combine.

4. Drain the tomatoes and peel away the skins. Chop the tomato flesh, then add all the tomatoes, including the juices, to the spice mix along with the water and tomato paste, and cook, covered, on a medium heat for 1 hour.

5. Now add the dates, orzo and stock, then cook gently, without the lid (to help the sauce thicken), for another 30 minutes on a medium heat. Make sure to stir occasionally so the pasta doesn't stick to the base of the pan.

6. Meanwhile, preheat the oven to 200°C/180°C fan/gas 6.

7. Brush the pitta breads with the melted butter and season with rock salt. Lay them flat on a baking tray and bake for 20 minutes, turning them over after 10.

8. Take the tagine off the heat and stir in the coriander and parsley. Serve with the crisp pitta breads.

PREP 20 MINUTES
COOK 1 HOUR 45 MINUTES

6 tomatoes (about 525g)

4 tablespoons olive oil

800g boneless goat meat (leg is ideal), cut into small chunks

2 cloves of garlic, crushed and finely chopped

1 medium onion, finely chopped

1 teaspoon salt

1 teaspoon ground cinnamon

1 teaspoon ground ginger

1 teaspoon paprika

50ml water

1 tablespoon tomato paste

125g pitted dates, kept whole

100g orzo pasta

200ml chicken stock

4 pitta breads, sliced into 2½cm strips

50g butter, melted

rock salt, for seasoning

a large handful of fresh coriander and parsley, chopped

HAGGIS TARTE TATIN

Serves 4

I was brought up on traditional Bangladeshi food, and my dad made sure to teach us about where meat came from and encouraged us to eat every possible part of the animal without being squeamish, ever! So I am not averse to the idea of eating haggis, and was curious to find a way to use this Scottish ingredient in my cooking. I do like to break the rules, though, so I've decided to use a vegetarian version of haggis, which means that those who are squeamish – or vegetarian – can still enjoy this recipe. A tarte tatin is simply a tart made upside down – this one has a simple pastry base topped with haggis and sweet shallots. It's something a bit different, and is delicious served with a creamy garlic dip and a simple green salad.

PREP 20 MINUTES

COOK 50 MINUTES

320g ready-rolled puff pastry

3 small to medium banana shallots, peeled and cut in half lengthways

3 tablespoons olive oil

250g vegetarian haggis

2 tablespoons unsalted butter

½ teaspoon salt

1 tablespoon dark brown sugar

3 tablespoons balsamic vinegar

1 egg, lightly beaten

1 sprig of fresh thyme, leaves picked

3 or 4 fresh chive flowers, to garnish (optional)

green salad, to serve

For the dip

100g full-fat soft cheese

50g Greek yoghurt

salt and pepper, for seasoning

1 large handful of fresh chives, finely chopped

1. Unroll your puff pastry on a board and place a 20cm non-stick ovenproof frying pan upside down on top of it. Cut out a circle, using the pan as a guide and making your circle about 2½cm bigger. Put the pastry back on the paper it was wrapped in and leave to chill in the fridge.

2. Preheat the oven to 200°C/180°C fan/gas 6.

3. Make sure the 6 shallot halves will fit neatly into your frying pan. Trim the non-root ends if necessary to make them fit together into a star shape, fanning out from the middle of the pan to look like the petals of a flower. Don't leave them in the pan at this stage – set them aside.

4. Put 1 tablespoon of oil into the frying pan and place on a medium heat. Add the crumbled haggis and cook on a medium heat for about 5 minutes, until slightly crispy. Remove and place in a bowl.

5. Add the remaining oil and the butter to the pan, and once the butter has melted add the shallots, cut side down, and cook over a low to medium heat for about 15 minutes, until they have softened but are still holding their shape. Every now and again, spoon a little of the butter and oil over the tops of the shallots as they cook.

6. Add the salt, sugar and balsamic and cook for 10 minutes on a low to medium heat, until the shallots are sticky and the sugar and vinegar have turned into a sweet caramel.

7. With the shallots arranged in their star shape, return the haggis to the pan, using it to fill the gaps between the shallots, then take the pan off the heat.

8. Take your pastry circle out of the fridge and place it on top of the shallot and haggis mixture. The circle will be bigger than the pan, so tuck the edges down the sides and under the mixture. It doesn't have to be perfect – the rustic nature is what makes it look good when you turn it out.

9. Brush all over the pastry with the beaten egg, then, using a sharp knife, prick 5 or 6 holes in the pastry. This will allow the steam to release itself and the pastry to puff up. Bake in the oven for 20–25 minutes.

10. Meanwhile, make the dip by mixing all the ingredients together in a small bowl.

11. As soon as the tart is cooked, turn it out of the pan immediately on to a plate so that the pastry lid now becomes the base. Garnish with the thyme leaves, and with the chive flowers separated into smaller buds, and serve with the dip and a green salad.

BOLOGNESE PIE

Serves 6–8

I love a hybrid bake. The kind that takes the elements of one dish but presents them differently. They do say, 'If it ain't broke, don't fix it,' but I like to swap things around and see how treating ingredients differently can change, enhance or amplify a dish's original flavour and texture. My bolognese pie fuses two classics – spaghetti and pie – and creates a crust using the spaghetti with bolognese as the filling. It ain't broke, it didn't need fixing, but I did it anyway.

PREP 40 MINUTES
COOK 1 HOUR 30 MINUTES

For the bolognese

4 tablespoons olive oil

4 rashers (bacon or halal turkey), chopped

2 cloves of garlic, finely chopped

2 onions, diced

1 teaspoon salt

2 carrots (approx. 200g), peeled and diced

2 celery sticks (approx. 150g), diced

1 teaspoon paprika

1 tablespoon ground cumin

500g beef mince

2 x 400g tins of chopped tomatoes

200g Cheddar cheese, grated

For the spaghetti crust

25g unsalted butter

25g plain flour

600ml whole milk, hot

salt and pepper, for seasoning

20g mature Cheddar cheese, grated

375g dried spaghetti

1. For the bolognese, place a large sauté pan on a medium heat. Add the oil and the chopped rashers and cook for about 5 minutes, until the rashers are crisp.

2. Add the garlic, onions, salt, carrots and celery and cook for another 5 minutes.

3. Add the paprika, cumin and beef mince and cook until the mince is brown and most of the liquid has evaporated. This should take about 15 minutes.

4. Pour in the chopped tomatoes and 300ml of water and cook for 30 minutes on a low to medium heat, until the bolognese sauce has thickened.

5. While the sauce is simmering, put the butter into a medium pan on a medium heat and let it melt.

6. Stir in the flour to create a roux, then cook for 1 minute. Slowly add the milk a little at a time, making sure to whisk continuously. You either need a second person helping or a very reliable jug that won't spill. I had neither, and an enormous clean-up job after.

7. Once all the milk is added, keep whisking until the sauce has thickened – this can take about 10 minutes. Season the sauce with salt and pepper, then take off the heat. Stir in the mature Cheddar.

8. Bring a large pan of water to the boil and add a large pinch of salt. Cook the spaghetti according to the packet instructions, then drain it and put back into the pan. Stir in the cheese sauce.

9. Preheat the oven to 190°C/170°C fan/gas 5.

10. Spread the spaghetti in the base of a large, deep, rectangular serving dish, approx. 20 x 30cm, making sure to tease the pasta up the sides of the dish. Fill the cavity in the centre with the bolognese and top with the grated Cheddar.

11. Bake for 25–30 minutes, until the base and top are crisp.

SUMAC LAMB CHOPS WITH CRUSHED CARAMELIZED ONION POTATOES

Serves 4

These chops are perfect for a barbecue. The lamb is grilled simply and the sumac does all the talking on the hot cooked chops, imparting an earthy, tangy flavour. Perfect paired with these crushed sweet caramelized potatoes, which can be eaten warm, or cold straight out of the fridge.

PREP 20 MINUTES

COOK 35 MINUTES

For the chops

1kg lamb chops

5 tablespoons olive oil

2 teaspoons salt

2–3 tablespoons sumac

For the crushed potatoes

1kg potatoes, peeled and cut into 2cm cubes

4 tablespoons olive oil

2 large onions (approx. 400g), sliced

¼ teaspoon salt

1 teaspoon light brown sugar

1. Put the potatoes into a large pan with plenty of water and a good teaspoon of salt. Bring to the boil, then cook for 1–2 minutes, until the potatoes are tender. Drain and throw back into the pan.

2. Using a mallet, bash the meat to thin it out. Put the chops on a tray or plate, drizzle them with the oil and season well with salt.

3. Place a non-stick pan on a high heat and cook the chops for 3 minutes on both sides. Once the chops are cooked, place them on a baking tray and sprinkle them on both sides with the sumac. Cover with foil and keep them warm.

4. Wipe any burnt bits from the pan, then add the oil and let it heat up on a medium heat. Add the onions, salt and sugar, and cook until the onions are golden, caramelized and soft. This should take 15 minutes.

5. Crush the potatoes lightly with the back of a fork and add to the onions. Mix through, then cook until the potatoes are warmed through and the edges are just crisp. Serve with the chops.

BEEF WELLINGTON
WITH FENNEL & MINT SALAD

Serves 5

For me, something like beef Wellington always seemed like such a far-fetched idea when I watched my favourite celebrity chefs make it on television. Even once I'd decided to have a go, and ventured out to buy a fillet of beef, it sat in my fridge until it had to be either cooked or thrown away. So I pushed myself and here I am, and I can reassure you that it is not as scary as it sounds or looks on the telly. A few simple steps is all it takes, and I promise I won't make you do the pastry from scratch either. So you can have time to breathe and pat yourself on the back. It's served with a very simple fennel salad which complements it nicely.

1. Preheat the oven to 200°C/180°C fan/gas 6.

2. Place the beef in a roasting dish, brush with olive oil all over and season. Roast in the oven for 25 minutes.

3. Meanwhile put the butter, garlic and onion into a medium pan and cook for 10 minutes. Then add the salt, mushrooms, fenugreek and water and cook for another 15 minutes, until all the liquid has evaporated.

4. Add the mustard to the mushroom mixture and set aside on a plate in the fridge to chill.

5. Take the beef fillet out of the oven and place in a dish. Chill in the fridge for 30 minutes, or until completely cold.

6. Divide the block of pastry into two pieces, one about 200g and the other 300g. Roll out the smaller block into an 18 x 30cm rectangle. Roll out the other block into a 28 x 36cm rectangle.

7. Note that beef fillets do vary in size, so the key is to have the base piece of pastry large enough to sit the fillet on with a gap of at least 2.5cm around the edges. The top piece then needs to be larger, as it has to cover the top and sides of the fillet but still with 2.5cm excess around the edges. Bear this in mind when rolling out the pastry and adjust to suit your meat if necessary.

8. Put the pastry in the fridge while you prepare everything else.

9. On a large piece of cling film, line up the rashers side by side, leaving no gaps. Spread the cold mushroom mix all over the rashers in an even layer.

Recipe continues overleaf →

**PREP 1 HOUR, PLUS CHILLING
COOK 1 HOUR**

1kg beef fillet

4 tablespoons olive oil

50g unsalted butter

1 clove of garlic, chopped

1 small onion (approx. 150g), finely chopped

¼ teaspoon salt, plus more for seasoning

250g button mushrooms, finely chopped (to resemble large breadcrumbs – this is best done by pulsing in a food processor)

2 tablespoons dried fenugreek leaves

100ml water

1 tablespoon English mustard

500g puff pastry

12 turkey rashers (I use the halal variety) or 12 slices of prosciutto

1 egg yolk, lightly beaten

2 tablespoons milk

a pinch of rock salt

For the fennel and mint salad

1 bulb of fennel (approx. 300g), core removed, thinly sliced

juice of ½ a lemon

1 small red onion (approx. 150g), thinly sliced

¼ teaspoon fine rock salt

a large handful of fresh mint (approx. 20g), roughly chopped

2 tablespoons olive oil

rocket leaves (approx. 90g)

10. Put the beef fillet in the centre, across the layer of rashers. Using the cling film, wrap the rashers and mushroom mix around the beef fillet, encasing it completely and using the rashers to keep it all secure.

11. Roll tightly into a sausage shape, using the cling film, and make sure to secure the ends by twisting. Place in the fridge for at least an hour, for the shape to firm up.

12. Place the smaller rectangle of pastry on a baking tray. Unroll the beef fillet from the cling film and place on top of the pastry.

13. Lightly whisk the egg yolk and milk together and brush the edges of the pastry with it. Then place the larger piece of pastry on top and tease it around the fillet, starting from the top, making sure to remove any air.

14. Seal the edges by pressing down firmly with the back of a fork. At this point, neaten the edges by cutting, if you need to. Using the back of a knife, score the top of the pastry without cutting right through. Brush the pastry all over with the egg mixture, then sprinkle with salt and place in the fridge for 3 hours (or overnight, if you're making it in advance).

15. Preheat the oven to 200°C/180°C fan/gas 6 and put a baking tray in to heat up. Once the tray is hot, take it out of the oven and place the fillet on the hot tray, on a sheet of baking paper.

16. Bake for 25 minutes for medium rare or 30 minutes for medium. Leave to stand for 15 minutes before slicing.

17. To make the salad, prepare the fennel by removing the hard tops. Slice thinly using a knife or a mandolin. Squeeze the lemon juice over the sliced fennel and put into a bowl.

18. Add the onion, salt and mint to the salad and, using your hands, squeeze the mixture to release some of the juices. Add the olive oil and mix through, then add the rocket leaves and mix with your hands.

19. Cut the Wellington into thick slices and serve with the salad.

TANDOORI SEEKH KEBABS WITH COCONUT RICE

Serves 6

I grew up on seekh kebabs, though not the kind you buy at the local takeaway, but the kind my dad used to bring home from his restaurant. Beautiful minced beef, spiced and cooked in a burning hot tandoor. Nothing can quite recreate the exact experience at home, but let's do what we can. We may not have a tandoor, but we have an oven and a cupboard full of spices.

PREP 30 MINUTES
COOK 40 MINUTES

For the seekh kebabs

1 large onion (about 200g), finely chopped

2 green chillies, finely chopped

3 tablespoons finely chopped fresh coriander

5 cloves of garlic, crushed

25g fresh ginger, peeled and crushed in a pestle and mortar

2 teaspoons cumin seeds

2 teaspoons garam masala

2 teaspoons salt

800g beef mince

5 tablespoons olive oil

For the coconut rice

1 tablespoon butter

1 tablespoon sunflower oil

1 large onion (approx. 200g), chopped

500g basmati rice

400ml coconut milk

600ml water

salt, for seasoning

1. Preheat the oven to 180C/160C fan/gas 4 and line a baking tray with baking paper.

2. Put the onion, chillies, coriander, garlic, ginger, cumin, garam masala, salt and beef mince into a bowl and mix together using your hands.

3. Using wet hands, divide the mixture into twelve equal mounds and shape them into seekh kebab sausage shapes. Place on the prepared baking tray and brush all over with the oil.

4. Bake for 25–30 minutes, making sure to turn them halfway.

5. For the rice, place a large non-stick pan on a medium heat and add the butter and oil. Add the onion and cook down for 5–10 minutes, until soft.

6. Add the rice and cook for 2 minutes on a high heat.

7. Add the coconut milk and water, and season with salt.

8. Bring to the boil, then allow to simmer for about 15–20 minutes, until all the liquid has evaporated.

9. Take the pan off the heat, put the lid on top and leave the rice to steam for another 5 minutes.

10. Serve the rice alongside the kebabs.

EASY CHICKEN TIKKA MASALA
WITH BASMATI RICE

Serves 3–4

I invited a playground mum over to my house a few years ago and fretted over what to cook for her children, who had never eaten a curry in their lives. I assured her I could do non-ethnic foods and would cook whatever her kids liked, but she insisted they would eat whatever I made, which I suspect was her way of introducing her kids to curry in the safety of a home and not in full public view of a packed Indian restaurant! So I set about creating the simplest and most delicious chicken tikka, with all the vibrancy but none of the food colouring or heat. Her kids loved it and have since refused to eat curries at restaurants because they don't taste like my tikka masala. Praise indeed!

1. Put the oil into a large pan and place on a medium heat. Add the crushed ginger and garlic and cook for about 1 minute.

2. Add the onions, salt and tomato purée and cook for about 5 minutes, until the onions have softened.

3. Add the chicken breast, garam masala and curry powder. Cook for 15 minutes. Add the water now, as the chicken will be starting to stick slightly. Cook until all the moisture has evaporated.

4. Now add the tomato soup, bring to the boil and leave to simmer on a low to medium heat for 25 minutes.

5. Take off the heat and add the chopped coriander.

6. To cook the rice, put it into a large non-stick pan with the water. Bring to the boil, then allow to simmer for about 10 minutes, until all the water has evaporated.

7. Turn the heat down completely, place a lid on the pan and allow the rice to steam gently for about 10 minutes.

8. Once the rice is cooked, use a fork to fluff it up. Then add the melted ghee and stir through. Serve with the tikka masala.

PREP 30 MINUTES
COOK 1 HOUR

For the tikka masala

5 tablespoons olive oil

30g fresh ginger, peeled and crushed

5 cloves of garlic, peeled and crushed

2 small onions (approx. 200g), finely chopped

1 teaspoon salt

1 tablespoon tomato purée

700g chicken breast, diced

1 tablespoon garam masala

1 tablespoon curry powder

100ml water

1 x 400g tin of tomato soup

a large handful of fresh coriander (30g), chopped

For the rice

375g basmati rice

830ml water

2 tablespoons ghee, melted

CRISPY CHICKEN WITH SWEET POTATO FRIES & BARBECUE BEANS

Serves 4

The first chicken and chip shop that ever opened in Luton is the same place where I still get my chicken and chips. I know it's my home and I am biased, but they are a force to be reckoned with! When I can't make it there, I like to create my own variations of my favourites at home. This crispy chicken has a hidden layer of spice and a crisp exterior, and is accompanied by baked sweet potato fries and warm barbecue beans.

PREP 30 MINUTES
COOK 1 HOUR

For the chicken

4 large pieces of chicken thigh (about 150g each), skin on and bone still in

200ml sweet chilli sauce

150g plain flour

1 teaspoon baking powder

1 teaspoon cayenne pepper

1 teaspoon onion powder

1 teaspoon garlic powder

1 teaspoon salt

150ml vegetable oil, for frying

For the sweet potato fries

2 large sweet potatoes (approx. 800g), cut into wedges

2 teaspoons garlic powder

1½ teaspoons paprika

a large pinch of salt

2 tablespoons olive oil

For the barbecue beans

2 x 400g tins of baked beans

1 teaspoon smoked paprika

2 tablespoons brown sauce

1. Put a large pan of water on the stove, add a large pinch of salt and bring to the boil. Add the chicken and boil for 15 minutes. Once boiled, place on kitchen paper and drain off the excess water.

2. Put the chicken in a bowl with the sweet chilli sauce. Set aside.

3. Put the flour, baking powder, cayenne pepper, onion powder, garlic powder and salt on a plate and mix together.

4. Dip each piece of chicken into the dry spice mix and set aside on another plate.

5. Heat the oil in a non-stick frying pan. Add the pieces of chicken and fry for 3 minutes on either side, until golden brown. Place on a baking tray.

6. Preheat the oven to 180°C/160°C fan/gas 4.

7. Combine the garlic powder, paprika and salt in a small bowl.

8. Put the sweet potato wedges on a large baking tray, then cover them with the garlic mix and drizzle with the oil.

9. Place the trays of chicken and sweet potatoes in the oven, with the sweet potatoes at the top, and bake for 25–30 minutes.

10. Meanwhile, mix together the beans, smoked paprika and brown sauce and gently heat them up.

11. Serve everything together, and dig in.

Party Time

I don't often have enormous parties. Not because I dislike company, as in fact I think there is nothing nicer than spending hours in a room full of friends talking about anything and everything. And not because I don't like feeding people, because (if I may say so myself!) that's the one talent I do have. It's also not because I don't like to be in the kitchen, because that is my favourite place to be. No, the reason I don't often have big parties is because I hate the idea of clearing up afterwards. The very thought of it completely puts me off. But every now and again common sense prevails and I realize I like nothing more than talking, feeding people and cooking nice things, so I throw a party and face my fear. And in the end, when faced with that dreaded clear-up after everyone's gone, it's normally not as bad as I thought it would be. Especially as it turns out I am very good at convincing my husband that he is the best clearer-upper in the whole wide world. (Works every time!) So in the spirit of having big parties more often, this chapter is full of my favourite recipes for a large turnout. Some are a bit more advanced than others, but they all make for a great party!

BLOODY MARY CASHEWS

Makes 1 large bowlful

I don't actually drink alcohol, so it may come as a surprise to see one of my recipes labelled 'Bloody Mary'. But the fact I don't drink doesn't take away my curiosity for the flavours used in cocktails and what makes them taste the way they do, and I enjoy nothing better than inventing new food-drink hybrids! Bloody Mary is a combination of sweet and savoury with a hint of chilli. I have had a virgin version of the classic and liked it a lot, so here I have tried to recreate the flavour in my party cashews.

PREP 20 MINUTES
COOK 2 MINUTES

4 teaspoons paprika

zest of 4 limes

4 teaspoons celery salt

2 egg whites

600g whole cashews

1. Preheat the oven to 200°C/180° fan/gas 5. Have a large baking tray ready.

2. Mix the paprika, lime zest and celery salt in a small bowl and set aside.

3. Put the egg whites into a large bowl and whisk for a few minutes by hand, until the mixture is light and frothy.

4. Add the nuts to the bowl of egg-white and mix through, making sure the nuts are covered with the egg white mixture. This acts as a glue for the spices to stick to.

5. Spread the cashews on the baking tray. Sprinkle over all the spice mixture, then, using a clean spoon, mix the nuts around so they are completely coated.

6. Bake in the oven for 10–12 minutes, making sure to give them a stir halfway through. Keep a close eye on them so they don't catch. You will know they are ready when the spices on the nuts are dry to the touch.

7. Take the cashews out of the oven and leave to cool on the tray. Once completely cool, put them into a large bowl or smaller bowls to serve.

CRAB SUMMER ROLLS

Makes 16

Unlike spring rolls, which are wrapped in pastry and deep-fried, summer rolls are wrapped in rice paper and don't need cooking, which makes them both easier and healthier. They are a feast for the eyes, not just the belly, since the translucent rice paper lets all the crunchy veg shine through, and the more colours you use, the better the rolls look – quite literally a rainbow on a plate. This makes all the difference. The trick to getting these spot on is to prepare everything at the start before assembling.

1. Chop all the vegetables and lay them out ready to assemble.

2. Put the crabmeat in a bowl and mix in the lemon zest. Set aside.

3. Boil a full kettle of water. Pour some into a shallow bowl – deep enough to entirely dunk one wrapper. Let the water cool a little.

4. Have ready a chopping board and a plate for your finished rolls. Dunk a wrapper into the warm water, completely submerging it. As soon as you feel it soften, take out and lay it flat on the board.

5. Place a few coriander leaves at one end of the wrapper. This will be the top of the roll when you are finished, and it's lovely to see the coriander leaves displayed. Now add a little bit of the onion, remembering that less is more. When laying out the vegetables, keep them within the shape of an 8cm rectangle – too big and you won't be able to roll the wrapper up comfortably.

6. Add the mangetout, carrot, pepper and crabmeat, then season. Now fold in the two sides of the wrapper to create two straight edges. Turn over the bottom of the wrapper to completely conceal the crab and veg, then roll the whole thing up, making sure to tuck in the sides as you go, keeping the shape of the roll.

7. Place on a tray, then repeat with the rest of the wrappers and filling. If you are not serving your summer rolls straight away, leave them in the fridge, covered with damp kitchen paper.

8. For the dipping sauce, mix together the lime juice and 1 tablespoon of sugar. Stir well until the sugar has dissolved. Add 1 tablespoon of fish sauce and mix. Taste, adding a little more sugar or fish sauce as needed. You want to balance the flavours so that no ingredient is more powerful than the others.

9. Mix in the ginger and as much chopped chilli as you like. Stir, taste and adjust the flavours if necessary.

PREP 25 MINUTES
NO COOK

1 small red onion, very thinly sliced

10 mangetout, very thinly sliced

1 small carrot, peeled and sliced into thin strips

1 small red pepper, thinly sliced

200g crabmeat (tinned or fresh)

zest of 1 lemon

16 spring roll wrappers

a large handful of fresh coriander, leaves picked

salt, for seasoning

For the dipping sauce

juice of 4 limes

1–1½ tablespoons palm sugar, golden caster sugar or coconut sugar

1–1½ tablespoons fish sauce, to taste

2cm piece of fresh ginger, peeled and finely chopped

½–1 large red chilli, finely chopped, to taste

CHEESE & CRYSTALLIZED GINGER STRAWS

Makes 18–20

Cheese straws used to be my go-to food for when I was out with the kids. It was what I gave them when carrot sticks no longer did the job. But they can be so much more than just a snack in a ziplock bag. They can be quite grown-up too! I love making cheese straws, because I can freeze them halfway through and later bake them from frozen. These are flavoured with Parmesan, and with a hidden surprise of crystallized ginger running through them. I can't decide if they are sweet or savoury, so I guess they can be either/or, or both.

PREP 40 MINUTES
COOK 15 MINUTES

1 x 320g pack of ready-rolled puff pastry

a little plain flour, for dusting

170g Parmesan cheese, finely grated

100g crystallized ginger, roughly chopped

1 egg, lightly beaten

a large pinch of rock salt

1. Preheat the oven to 220°C/200°C fan/gas 7. Line a baking tray with baking paper.

2. Place the ready-rolled puff pastry on a lightly floured work surface. Sprinkle one half of the pastry with half the grated Parmesan and all the chopped crystallized ginger. Fold over the other half of the pastry and press down firmly.

3. Roll the whole thing out to about the thickness of a pound coin, trying to keep it a rectangle shape as much as you can.

4. Using a pizza cutter, cut the pastry into 1cm strips. Brush the tops of the strips with the beaten egg and sprinkle with the rest of the Parmesan. Place them on the baking tray and twist them a few times, then sprinkle with salt.

5. If you like, you can freeze them at this point – keep them on the baking tray and place it in the freezer, so they don't lose their shape. Once they're frozen, keep them in a ziplock bag in the freezer till you are ready to bake them.

6. Bake on the middle shelf of the oven for 10–12 minutes, or until golden and crisp. If you are baking them from frozen, they will take 15–17 minutes at the same temperature.

7. Take out of the oven and leave to cool on the tray.

8. These will keep in an airtight container for three days if you want to make them in advance.

ARANCINI BALLS WITH
ROASTED RED PEPPER & PINE NUT DIP

Makes 10

These delicious morsels are essentially balls of smooth, sticky rice inside a crisp shell. They are a great way to use up leftover risotto, though I do often cook risotto especially for them. Once you have cooled the rice, it is yours to flavour with whatever you want. I like the strong taste of cheese with the zing of chives.

1. Put the stock in a large pan with the saffron. Bring to the boil.

2. Add the risotto rice and the salt and bring back to the boil, then lower the temperature and leave to simmer and cook until the rice has absorbed all the liquid, about 30 minutes.

3. Take off the heat, stir in both types of cheese and allow to melt, then add the chives and spread out the rice on a flat tray. Once the rice has cooled to room temperature, place it in the fridge for about 1 hour to cool completely.

4. Meanwhile, to make the dip, put the roasted red peppers into a food processor and add the cumin, oil, pine nuts, garlic and balsamic vinegar. Blitz the mixture to a smooth paste and transfer to a serving bowl. Set aside until ready to serve.

5. Remove the rice from the fridge, then wet your hands and make the mixture into 10 equal balls.

6. Make a batter by putting the egg, flour, salt, garlic powder and water into a bowl and mixing to a smooth paste.

7. Heat the oil to 170°C, or until a breadcrumb dropped into the oil sizzles and rises to the top. Working in batches of a few at a time, dip each rice ball first into the batter, then into the breadcrumbs, and fry for 4–5 minutes, turning them around, until they are a golden brown. Drain on kitchen paper.

8. Serve the arancini hot with the dip.

PREP 2 HOURS 45 MINUTES
COOK 15 MINUTES

For the arancini

800ml vegetable stock

a good pinch of saffron

250g risotto rice

½ teaspoon salt

50g Parmesan cheese, finely grated

150g mozzarella, grated

30g fresh chives, finely chopped

1 medium egg

170g plain flour

½ teaspoon fine salt

1 teaspoon garlic powder

200ml water

vegetable oil, for frying

500g fine breadcrumbs

For the dip

1 x 340 jar of roasted red peppers, drained

1 teaspoon ground cumin

5 tablespoons olive oil

75g pine nuts

1 clove of garlic

1 tablespoon balsamic vinegar

SALMON SCOTCH EGGS

— Makes 20 wedges —

Scotch eggs needn't just be for picnics, they can be for parties that take place indoors too! This is not too different to a regular Scotch egg recipe, except that I've chosen to wrap the eggs in something else – here they are encased in pink salmon, which is delicately flavoured with dill and onion seeds.

PREP 50 MINUTES

COOK 25 MINUTES

5 hard-boiled eggs, peeled

½ tablespoon plain flour

4 large skinless salmon fillets (645g),

2 spring onions, roughly chopped

½ a packet of fresh dill (15g), roughly chopped, plus extra to garnish

2 teaspoons onion seeds

6 tablespoons fresh breadcrumbs

½ teaspoon salt

1 teaspoon black pepper

mayonnaise, to serve

1. Dry the hard-boiled eggs with kitchen paper, then roll them in the flour until they are lightly coated. This will help the salmon stick to the egg.

2. Put the salmon into a food processor and add the spring onions and dill. Blitz until you have a smooth paste. Transfer the paste to a bowl and add the onion seeds, breadcrumbs, salt and pepper.

3. Preheat the oven to 200°C/180°C fan/gas 6 and lightly grease a baking tray.

4. Divide the salmon into 5 equal portions. Flatten each one, put an egg in the middle, then press the fish around the edges, encasing the egg.

5. Place on the baking tray, and repeat with the rest of the eggs. Bake the Scotch eggs in the oven for 30 minutes, then take out and allow to cool completely.

6. Slice each cooled Scotch egg into 4 wedges, arrange on a serving plate and garnish with dill. Serve with mayo.

CARAWAY PITTA CHIPS
WITH BEETROOT & FETA DIP

Serves 8–10

I love nothing better than opening a packet and pouring out the contents into the biggest bowl I can find. I think we all have times when we want to do as little as possible. But we also all have times when we want to show off, and this recipe is for those extra-effort days. It's a simple method, but really delivers on colour and flavour, combining aromatic pitta chips with a deliciously easy beetroot dip.

1. For the pitta chips, begin by toasting the caraway seeds lightly in a non-stick pan, being careful not to burn them as this will make them bitter. As soon as you hear a few sounds of popping, take them off the heat and crush them to a fine powder, using a pestle and mortar or a spice grinder.

2. Put the olive oil into a bowl. Stir in the crushed caraway seeds.

3. Preheat the oven to 180°C/160°C fan/gas 4. Have a large baking tray ready.

4. Using a small sharp knife, separate each pitta to make 2 ovals. Now slice the ovals into wedges or strips (I like strips). Brush the strips with the oily spice mix and place on the baking tray, making sure there is not too much overlap. If you find that there is, use a second tray or bake them in batches. Sprinkle with salt.

5. Bake in the oven for 18–20 minutes, until the chips are a light golden brown and crisp. Keep an eye on them, as they may cook slightly quicker.

6. Take them out of the oven and leave to cool. Once cooled they can be stored in an airtight container for few weeks. But set aside if you are using them the same day.

7. Meanwhile, to make the dip, put the beetroot into a food processor, along with the oil, salt, garlic and a squeeze of lemon juice, and blitz to a smooth paste.

8. Transfer the dip to a serving bowl and crumble on some feta before serving. I like to drizzle it with a little bit more olive oil, too. Serve with the pitta chips.

PREP 45 MINUTES
COOK 20 MINUTES

For the caraway pitta chips
3 teaspoons caraway seeds

75ml olive oil

6 pitta breads (white or wholemeal)

a large pinch of salt

For the beetroot dip
500g cooked beetroot (not the kind in vinegar – be sure to check)

3 tablespoons olive oil, plus extra for drizzling

a pinch of salt, to taste

2 cloves of garlic

a squeeze of lemon juice

150g feta cheese

SUMAC & LEMON THYME FOCACCIA

Makes 2 (serves 8–10)

Bread was the one thing that I used to be afraid of where baking was concerned. It took many a disaster before I really began to understand the process. I still have much to learn, but one of my favourite breads that I've learnt to bake on this journey of bread discovery is focaccia. I particularly like this sumac and thyme version, which is so moist that it really doesn't need anything else served alongside it.

PREP 1 HOURS 50 MINUTES, INCLUDING PROVING
COOK 18 MINUTES

500g strong bread flour, plus extra 75g if making by hand

2 teaspoons salt

14g fast action yeast

2 tablespoons olive oil, plus extra for drizzling

400ml cold water

2 large sprigs of lemon thyme, leaves picked

a large pinch of rock salt

2 tablespoons sumac

1. Place the flour in a large mixing bowl or the bowl of a stand mixer. Add the salt to one side of the bowl and the yeast to the opposite side.

2. Add the olive oil and water and mix to bring the dough together. If you are using a stand mixer, attach the dough hook and knead on high for 5 minutes. If you are kneading by hand, lightly grease the surface of your worktop and knead for 10 minutes. The dough will be quite sticky at first, so if you are kneading by hand you may need to add up to 75g more flour to help make it workable.

3. The dough should now be smooth and stretchy. Place it in a greased bowl, cover and leave to double in size. This could take an hour, sometimes less, sometimes more, depending on how warm your room is.

4. Once the dough has doubled in size, turn it out on to a work surface and divide it in half.

5. Place a piece of dough on a large flat baking tray, then grease your hands and push the dough out to cover as much of the tray as possible.

6. Repeat with the second piece of dough, then cover both trays with greased cling film and leave for 1 hour.

7. Preheat the oven to 220°C/200°C fan/gas 7.

8. Get rid of the cling film, then, using your fingertips, press indents into the dough. Drizzle with plenty of olive oil, so you have puddles of oil in the indents you made. Sprinkle over the lemon thyme leaves and rock salt.

9. Bake for 15–18 minutes, swapping the two trays over halfway through cooking to ensure an even bake.

10. Once out of the oven, sprinkle over the sumac while the bread is still warm. I like to serve the focaccia with good olive oil and balsamic vinegar.

ASPARAGUS PIZZA BIANCO

Makes 2 large pizzas

'Asparagus on a pizza?' I hear you ask. Asparagus is such a delicious vegetable but it often gets overlooked among the jungle of other vegetables out there. So I wanted to make asparagus, with its delicate flavour and crisp texture, the star of the show! And what better way to do that than putting it on a pizza? If we're breaking rules, we might as well break them in style!

1. To make the pizza base, put the flour into a mixing bowl, with the yeast on one side of the bowl and the salt on the other.

2. Put the oil, warm milk and water into a jug. Add the wet mixture to the dry and mix together till a dough is formed.

3. Knead by hand for 10 minutes, or use a stand mixer with a dough hook attached for 5 minutes on a medium speed. The dough should be smooth and elastic. Leave it in the bowl, cover with cling film and place in a warm part of the house to double in size. This can take up to an hour, depending on how warm or cold it is.

4. Once doubled, take the dough out of the bowl and knock the air out. Divide into 2 equal mounds, place on a tray, cover and leave to rise again.

5. Meanwhile make the sauce. Put the cream into a small pan with the garlic and place on a medium heat until it has halved in quantity and is thicker, about 3–4 minutes. Take off the heat, add the Parmesan and rosemary, mix and set aside.

6. Heat the oven to 240°C/220°C fan/gas 9 and put two baking sheets in to heat up.

7. Lightly dust the work surface with flour. Roll out one piece of dough as thinly as you can, into a circle about 25cm wide. Repeat with the other piece.

8. Take the hot baking sheets out of the oven and carefully lift the pizza bases onto them. Spread half the creamy sauce all over each base, then divide the asparagus slices between them. Finally, sprinkle the cheese over both pizzas.

9. Bake for 10–12 minutes on the top and middle shelf, swapping the trays over halfway, until the topping is bubbling and golden and the bases are browned at the edges.

10. Lift the pizzas onto cutting boards, zest the lemon over the top, then slice and serve.

PREP 30 MINUTES,
PLUS RESTING
COOK 25 MINUTES

For the base

325g '00' pasta flour

1 teaspoon fast-action yeast

1 teaspoon salt

20ml olive oil

50ml warm milk

150ml warm water

For the topping

200ml double cream

3 cloves of garlic, crushed

40g Parmesan cheese, finely grated

1 sprig of fresh rosemary, leaves picked and finely chopped

100g mature Cheddar cheese, grated

250g asparagus, woody ends removed (to leave approx. 150g), thinly sliced lengthways

zest of 1 small lemon

BEEF CARPACCIO WITH GHEE BREAD

Makes 8

Most of my older relatives recoil at the thought of carpaccio. I was raised in a culture where everything has to be cooked to death, and I mean even down to the poor veg, which gets boiled to within an inch of its life. I've always rebelled and deliberately eaten anything that makes my elders reel. My dad is the one exception: he shares my opinion and welcomes carpaccio, tartare, anything that doesn't need much cooking, with simple flavours enhancing the star ingredient. To make carpaccio you need to use a really fresh cut of meat. I always buy it on the day I am going to use it. Here it's cooked lightly, with a mustard crust, then chilled and sliced before being served on a buttery ghee crispbread with a sharp salsa verde.

PREP 25 MINUTES
COOK 25 MINUTES

For the carpaccio

400g beef steak

salt, for seasoning

2 tablespoons English mustard powder

1 tablespoon olive oil, for frying

For the salsa verde

60g fresh mixed herbs (you can use whatever you like – I used mint, coriander, dill, chives and oregano)

2 cloves of garlic, peeled

1 tablespoon capers

2 anchovies

1 teaspoon French mustard

100ml olive oil

2 tablespoons apple cider vinegar

For the ghee toast

8 slices of tiger bread, thinly sliced

50g ghee, melted

1. Season the steak with salt and the mustard powder. Place a non-stick pan on a medium heat and add the oil. Fry the steak for 1 minute on each side, then take off the heat and leave to cool completely in the fridge.

2. Once the carpaccio has cooled, wrap it in cling film and place in the freezer for 3–4 hours. This will allow you to cut really thin slices.

3. Meanwhile, make the salsa verde: put all the ingredients into a food processor and blitz to a smooth paste.

4. Preheat the oven to 200°C/180°C fan/gas 6 and have a baking tray at the ready.

5. Brush both sides of the sliced bread with the melted ghee. Place on the baking tray and put into the oven for 18–20 minutes, or until the bread is golden and crisp. Take out and leave to cool.

6. To serve, take the carpaccio out of the freezer and remove the cling film. Slice really thinly and leave it to just come up to room temperature.

7. Top the bread with the sliced beef and drizzle with the salsa verde before serving.

PULLED BEEF IN BRIOCHE

Serves 6–8

Pulled meat, of any sort, has recently become very popular, especially at festivals and street food markets. I have tried so many variations, and everyone has their own way of doing it. I like my pulled meat to be stringy and tender, with a runny sauce that is just slightly thickened. I often cook mine in a slow cooker, but you can cook it equally well on the stovetop or in the oven. This recipe creates a delicious combination of sweet, sour and hot chilli, with freshness from the coriander scattered over at the end.

PREP 55 MINUTES

COOK 3 HOURS 5 MINUTES

3 tablespoons olive oil

800g beef (skirt steak, beef cheeks, shin or shoulder), in steaks or pieces

1 teaspoon of salt, plus more for seasoning

2 medium onions, chopped

3 cloves of garlic, crushed

1 x 400g tin of chopped tomatoes

2 tablespoons brown sauce

2 tablespoons runny honey

1 tablespoon balsamic vinegar

1 teaspoon smoked paprika

350ml beef stock

3 tablespoons sriracha chilli sauce

1 tablespoon cornflour, mixed with 2 tablespoons water

30g fresh coriander, roughly chopped

8–10 brioche buns, to serve

1. Put the olive oil into a large ovenproof crockpot or large non-stick frying pan, and place on a high heat. Season the beef with salt really well on all sides. Put the beef into the pot or pan and fry for a few minutes on each side, till the exterior is brown and crisp, then take out and set aside.

2. To the same pan add the onions, garlic and 1 teaspoon of salt, and cook until the onions are softened. Now add the chopped tomatoes, brown sauce, honey, vinegar and paprika and cook for 5 minutes on a medium heat, until the mixture has reduced and thickened.

3. If you are using the oven, preheat it to 180°C/160°C fan/gas 4.

4. If you are using the same crockpot, put the beef back into the pot. If you are using a slow cooker, put in the beef along with the cooked onion and tomato mixture. Pour over the beef stock and give it all a good stir.

5. For a slow cooker, cook on high for 3 hours. On the stovetop, cook with the lid on for 3 hours on a medium to low heat. If cooking in the oven, it will need 3 hours with the lid on.

6. Check the meat halfway through cooking – if the liquid is drying up too fast, lower the oven heat slightly and add another 100ml of water.

7. After 3 hours take the beef out and use two forks to pull it apart. Put the meat back into the pan. Stir in the sriracha and the cornflour paste, and cook for another 5 minutes.

8. Take off the heat and stir in the fresh coriander.

9. Serve the pulled beef with sliced brioche buns. Sandwich the meat in between the buns and give them a go.

OATCAKE, POTATO & DILL SAMOSAS

Makes 12

No matter where I am or what I'm doing, if I see a samosa I always want to know and taste what's inside. I have made it my life's mission to discover how many ways I can make a samosa, what I can fill it with and what I can wrap it in. The inspiration for these samosa cases is delicious Derbyshire oatcakes. Not the crisp kind you'll know from the cheeseboard, but more like a soft round savoury pancake. Here I've filled them with a lightly spiced potato and pea filling and fresh dill. If you can't find these oatcakes near where you live, you can substitute shop-bought pancakes instead – they will work exactly the same.

1. To make the filling, heat the oil in a non-stick frying pan on a medium heat, add the onion and salt, and cook until soft and lightly brown. Add the cumin and peas and cook for a few minutes.

2. Stir in the dill, along with the mashed potato, and make sure everything is nicely incorporated, then transfer the mixture to a bowl and leave to cool completely.

3. Line a baking tray with baking paper. Cut the oatcakes in half, to make 12 semi-circles.

4. Mix together the flour and water to make the 'glue'.

5. Take one of the oatcake semi-circles and put a heaped tablespoon of the filling in the centre, making sure not to get it around the edges.

6. Fold one side of the oatcake over the filling, then fold over the other side. Brush the seams with the 'glue', then the base. Press the edges together and place on the baking tray. Repeat with the rest of the oatcakes and filling.

7. Place the samosas in the freezer for 30 minutes.

8. Meanwhile, pour the oil into a medium pan and heat to 190°C. You will know the oil is ready for frying when you drop in some of the 'glue' and it sizzles and rises to the top. Fry a few samosas at a time, for a couple of minutes on each side, until they are crisp and golden.

9. Drain on kitchen paper, and serve warm.

PREP 30 MINUTES,
PLUS CHILLING
COOK 30 MINUTES

For the filling

1–2 tablespoons vegetable oil

1 large white onion,
finely chopped

1 teaspoon salt

2 teaspoons ground cumin

150g frozen peas, defrosted

25g fresh dill, finely chopped

400g mashed potato, cooled

6 Derbyshire oatcakes or
20cm shop-bought pancakes

2 litres vegetable oil

For the 'glue'

4 tablespoons plain flour

4 tablespoons water

LEMON & FENNEL MARINATED OLIVES

Makes 1 large bowlful

To me, no party is complete without a huge bowl of olives. I love the natural saltiness they bring, which cuts through everything else on the table. They are always a popular addition, and with this recipe I want to show that you don't have to buy expensive jars or posh ones from the deli. You can buy plain olives and jazz them up with your own flavours. These ones are laced with fennel, lemon and lots of olive oil.

PREP 25 MINUTES, PLUS MARINATING

1 bulb of fennel, with lots of fronds

4 tablespoons olive oil

3 cloves of garlic, crushed and finely chopped

1 teaspoon chilli flakes

2 teaspoons dried basil

1 teaspoon fennel seeds

zest of 1 lemon, plus a squeeze of lemon juice

a pinch of salt

550g mixed pitted olives

1. Finely chop the fennel fronds and set aside. Slice the fennel bulb – you only need 200g, so use any extra for another recipe.

2. Put the olive oil, garlic, chilli flakes and basil into a large bowl.

3. Toast the fennel seeds gently in a small pan on a medium heat till they start to pop, then take off the heat and crush the seeds. This will help to release their oils.

4. Add the fennel seeds and lemon zest to the bowl, along with a squeeze of lemon juice. Add a pinch of salt and give it all a good mix.

5. Stir in the sliced fennel and the fennel fronds, cover the bowl , and set aside for 30 minutes.

6. Mix in the olives, then cover and leave in the fridge until you are ready to use them.

SALT COD FRITTERS WITH PINK PEPPERCORN SAUCE

Makes 20

I cannot express how much I adore salt cod – although the first time I ever cooked with it, I committed a cardinal sin and went for the no-soak, no-boil, straight-out-of-the-packet type cooking method. I can see you wincing at the very thought. I paid for my mistake by way of wasted ingredients, but the looks on the kids' faces were priceless as they tasted it. So salt cod is to be treated with love and patience. It's the only way to get the best from this delicious preserved fish.

1. Place the salt cod, milk and sugar in a pan and bring to the boil. Remove and leave to cool, then place in the fridge to soak overnight.

2. Once cooled, remove any skin and bones and break the fish into flakes. Put into a large bowl with the mashed potato.

3. Put the olive oil into a small frying pan and place on a medium heat. Add the garlic and onion and cook gently for 5 minutes, until the onion is soft. Add the chilli flakes and cook for another 5 minutes. Let the mixture cool, then add to the potato and fish.

4. Add the lemon zest, chopped coriander and egg and give it all a good mix.

5. Shape the mixture into 20 equal-size fishballs and set aside on a board.

6. Heat the vegetable oil in a large pan. Test to see that it's hot enough by putting a tiny bit of the mixture into the pan – if it sizzles and comes to the surface, the oil is ready.

7. Place a few of the fishballs in the oil at a time, making sure to keep them moving. They will take 3–4 minutes to cook – you want them to be an even golden brown. Repeat in batches until you've cooked them all, draining them on kitchen paper.

8. To make the sauce, put the salad cream, lemon juice and pink peppercorns into a small bowl and mix together.

9. Serve the salt cod fritters with the sauce.

Tip: To make 300g of mash from scratch, cook 1 large (350g) floury potato for 10–15 minutes in the microwave in 5-minute bursts, then peel and mash the flesh.

Photograph overleaf →

PREP 40 MINUTES,
PLUS SOAKING
COOK 50 MINUTES

For the fritters

500g salt cod

800ml whole milk

2 tablespoons caster sugar

300g mashed potato, cooled
(see tip below)

1 tablespoon olive oil

1 clove of garlic, crushed

1 small onion (approx.
100g), chopped

1 teaspoon chilli flakes

zest of 1 lemon (save the
juice for the sauce)

a handful of fresh coriander
(approx. 20g), chopped

1 large egg

1–2 litres vegetable oil,
for frying, depending
on size of pan

For the sauce

6 tablespoons salad cream

juice of 1 lemon (see above)

2 tablespoons pink
peppercorns, crushed
to a fine powder

POPCORN MUSSELS WITH PAPRIKA CHIVE MAYO

Serves 4

I was left traumatized after my dad decided to cook a prawn mussel curry. He used to come home from his restaurant and cook up a storm, and among his other culinary creations he had tried currying herring roe, caviar, squid – and, on this occasion, mussels. After that, every time anyone asked me if I liked mussels I was quick to respond, 'I hate them.' But then I discovered beautiful cookbooks, which taught me how to cook mussels properly and treat them with respect. What I have learnt is that not everything needs to be curried. Especially not mussels. These popcorn mussels are deliciously crisp, with a sweet soft centre. The reason why I call them popcorn mussels is because that is exactly how we eat them – like popcorn. Once I start, I just cannot stop!

1. Check the mussels – if there are any that have broken shells or that won't open, discard them. Put the rest of the mussels into a large pan with 200ml of water. Put the lid on top and cook for 1 minute on a high heat.

2. Lower the heat to medium and continue to cook for another 3 minutes, then drain and leave to cool for few minutes.

3. Take out the mussel meat and place on a tray lined with kitchen paper to drain off excess moisture. If any mussels have not opened, just throw them away.

4. Tip the 130g of flour, the garlic powder, onion powder and baking powder into a bowl. Add the remaining 150ml of water and mix to a smooth paste.

5. Dust the mussel meat with the 50g of flour. Get rid of any excess flour, then put the mussel meat into the bowl with the paste and mix, making sure all the mussels are covered.

6. Heat the oil to 150°C, if you have a thermometer, otherwise drop in a bit of the batter – when it starts to sizzle and rise to the top, the oil is ready.

7. Fry the mussels in batches for 3–4 minutes. Drain on kitchen paper and sprinkle with salt.

8. To make the sauce, put the mayo, paprika, salt and chives into a bowl and mix together. Serve the sauce with the mussels.

PREP 30 MINUTES
COOK 20 MINUTES

For the mussels

1kg mussels, de-bearded and cleaned

350ml water

130g plain flour, plus 50g for dusting

¼ teaspoon garlic powder

1 teaspoon onion powder

¼ teaspoon baking powder

1.5 litres vegetable oil, for frying

salt, for seasoning

For the paprika chive mayo

7 tablespoons mayonnaise (approx. 105g)

½ teaspoon paprika

salt, for seasoning

a large handful of fresh chives, finely chopped

FENNEL WELSH CAKES WITH BLUEBERRY COULIS

Makes about 24

Whenever I visit Wales, I find myself so mesmerized by the view from the train window that I always nearly miss my stop. On my first trip there, wondering what I could take back for my children apart from a fridge magnet, the answer came when I discovered Welsh cakes! Shaped much like a scone, but flatter and cooked on a griddle, they are sweet and spicy, full of chewy currants. Back home, fridge magnet in hand, I set out to recreate this simple yet delicious treat for the kids. My version is spiced with crushed fennel seeds, dotted with tart dried blueberries, and served with a crisp, fresh blueberry coulis. In Wales, Welsh cakes are often eaten with butter and jam, so you can go more traditional if you prefer. Either way, these mini ones make a great sweet treat at a party.

PREP 45 MINUTES
COOK 20 MINUTES (COOK IN 2–3 BATCHES)

For the Welsh cakes

225g plain flour, plus extra for dusting

285g golden caster sugar

½ teaspoon baking powder

1 teaspoon fennel seeds, crushed

100g unsalted butter, cubed, plus extra for greasing

50g dried blueberries, roughly chopped

1 medium egg, lightly beaten

2 tablespoons whole milk

For the coulis

250g fresh blueberries

1 tablespoon icing sugar

a squeeze of lemon juice

1. Put the flour and 85g of the caster sugar into a large bowl, add the baking powder and crushed fennel seeds and mix together.

2. Add the cubed butter and use your fingertips to rub it in until the mixture resembles breadcrumbs.

3. Scatter the blueberries in and mix through, then make a well in the centre and add the egg. Use a palette knife to mix the egg in, then pour in the milk and get your hands in there to bring the dough together.

4. Dust your work surface with flour and roll out the dough to 1cm thickness. Using a 4cm round cutter, cut out rounds, then take all the scraps, bring them together and re-roll. Cut out more rounds, and keep doing this until you have used up all the dough.

5. Put the remaining 200g of caster sugar into a bowl.

6. Lightly brush a medium non-stick pan with a little melted butter. Or alternatively you can use spray oil.

7. Place a batch of Welsh cakes in the pan, well spaced out, and cook over a low heat for 3 minutes. Turn them over and cook for another 3 minutes, then take off the heat and immediately dip each Welsh cake into the bowl of sugar. Set aside.

8. Do the same for the remaining Welsh cakes: cook, coat in sugar and set aside.

9. To make the coulis, put the blueberries into a food processor with the icing sugar and lemon juice and blitz until broken down. Then push through a sieve to remove all the bits.

10. Serve the coulis in a small bowl alongside the Welsh cakes.

CITRUS LAMINGTONS
Makes 16 slices

Lamingtons are an Australian speciality that consists of two layers of cake sandwiched with a sweet filling, cut into bite-size squares, covered in chocolate and rolled in lots of coconut. Traditionalists may think I have massacred the recipe, but I say what's life without a little variation? I have kept my favourite bit – the desiccated coconut coating – but switched what's inside to a simple citrus madeira cake, with curd made out of the leftover tangy citrus juices. And in case I haven't changed things enough, my Lamingtons are triangular rather than square!

1. Preheat the oven to 180°C/160°C fan/gas 4, and line and grease a 20cm cake tin.

2. For the cake, beat the butter and sugar together, using a freestanding or hand-held mixer, for 10 minutes, until the mixture is really fluffy and almost white in colour.

3. Add the eggs gradually and incorporate well. Add the zest and flour and fold in. Finally, mix in the milk.

4. Pour the mixture into the prepared tin and level off the top. Bake for 45–50 minutes, until the cake is golden and a skewer inserted comes out clean.

5. Leave to cool in the tin for 10 minutes, then take out and cool on a wire rack. Once completely cold, wrap the cake in cling film and chill for 1 hour in the fridge. This makes it easier to cut neatly.

6. Meanwhile make the curd by putting the juice, sugar, butter, eggs, egg yolk and cornflour into a small non-stick pan on a medium heat. Whisk all the time, until the mixture is bubbling and has thickened. This will take about 5 minutes. Take off the heat and sieve into a bowl to remove any lumps.

7. Cover with cling film, making sure the film touches the top of the curd. This will stop a skin forming. Leave to cool completely.

8. Take the cake out of the fridge, unwrap and slice into 16 equal triangular wedges, using a sharp serrated knife.

9. Place the desiccated coconut on a flat plate.

10. Taking one piece of cake at a time, brush all over with the cooled curd (including the base), then press into the coconut, making sure all sides are generously covered.

Tip: The easiest and neatest way to cover and coat your Lamingtons is to brush the base, outer edge and top of each slice first, then dip into the coconut. Then do the inner sides one at a time.

PREP 55 MINUTES
COOK 50 MINUTES

For the cake
175g unsalted butter, softened

175g caster sugar

3 medium eggs, lightly beaten

zest of 1 lemon

zest of 1 orange

zest of 1 lime

250g self-raising flour, sifted

3 tablespoons whole milk

100g desiccated coconut

For the citrus curd
juice of the lemon, orange and lime (see above – the juice should make up 110ml)

150g caster sugar

75g unsalted butter, melted

2 medium eggs

1 egg yolk

1 teaspoon cornflour

MINI MILLIONAIRE'S CUPS

Makes 12

I've never been quite sure why millionaire's shortbread is so called, though I imagine it's because it is extremely rich! But wherever the name came from, you don't have to be rich to eat it, or to make it. With its crisp buttery base, topped with caramel and milk chocolate, it takes shortbread to a whole new dimension. This is my version of the biscuit-slash-dessert, but in individual cup-shaped portions. They are easy to make and even easier to serve because there's no cutting involved.

PREP 3½ HOURS,
INCLUDING COOLING
COOK 20 MINUTES

For the shortbread

125g unsalted butter, room temperature, plus extra for greasing

55g caster sugar

180g plain flour, plus extra for dusting

a pinch of salt

For the caramel

75g unsalted butter

75g soft brown sugar

½ x 397g tin of condensed milk

¼ teaspoon rock salt

For the chocolate

300g milk chocolate, melted

1. Preheat the oven to 190°C/170°C fan/gas 5.

2. Grease a standard cupcake tray and line the base of each cup with a small round of baking paper. I've found that a 5cm cutter fits the base of a standard cupcake tin, so I use that as a template to mark 12 circles on baking paper, then cut them out. Once the base is lined with the paper circles, grease again. Set aside.

3. Put the butter and sugar into a bowl and mix to a smooth paste. Add the flour and salt and bring the dough together. Wrap in cling film and leave to chill for 15 minutes in the fridge.

4. On a floured surface, roll out the dough to 1cm thickness. Using the same 5cm cutter used to make the paper circles, cut out some rounds. Take any trimmings and roll back together, then roll again and cut out more rounds. Do this till you have 12 rounds.

5. Place each round of dough in the base of a cupcake cup and push down against the edges of the tin. Prick the dough with a fork – this will stop the shortbread puffing up.

6. Bake for 16–18 minutes, until lightly golden brown. Leave to cool in the tin.

7. Meanwhile, make the caramel. Put the butter and sugar into a small non-stick pan, place on a medium heat and stir till the sugar dissolves. Add the condensed milk and keep stirring over a medium heat for 3-5 minutes till the mixture thickens and turns light golden brown. Take off the heat and mix in the rock salt.

8. Quickly add a tablespoon of caramel to each of the shortbread rounds and leave to set for 30 minutes.

9. Now put a tablespoon of melted chocolate on top of each shortbread round and chill in the fridge for 45 minutes.

10. Use a knife to gently run around the edge of each tin and take the millionaire's shortbreads out. Be sure to remove the baking paper from underneath.

SALTED PRETZEL & HAZELNUT BARK

Makes 1 large sheet

This bark may look complicated but it's essentially just melted chocolate scattered with toppings. Easy, right? And the more creative you get, the fancier it looks. So let your imagination run wild. This is my favourite combination – bitter dark chocolate and sweet white chocolate marbled together, with saltiness from the twisted pretzels and nuttiness from the roasted hazelnuts. It's lovely served as something sweet on the side, and also looks great broken into chaotic shards and used as decoration on top of a cake.

PREP 25 MINUTES

COOLING 2 HOURS

300g dark chocolate, melted

75g white chocolate, melted

75g salted pretzels, any size

20g roasted hazelnuts, chopped

1. Start by melting the dark chocolate. I like to do this in the microwave in short bursts, stirring in between, or you can melt the chocolate in a bain-marie set over a pan of simmering water.

2. Line a baking tray with baking paper. Spread the melted dark chocolate on the paper in a thin and even layer, but making sure not to spread the chocolate *too* thinly.

3. Now melt the white chocolate in the same way as before and immediately dollop drops of the melted white chocolate on to the dark, using a skewer to marble the top and run the two colours together. Don't be tempted to overdo it, or you will lose the marbled effect.

4. Now place the pretzels on top, making sure to push them in or they will pop out when you eventually cut the shards.

5. Sprinkle with the hazelnuts and leave to chill until the chocolate has set and is firm.

6. Using a sharp knife, cut the chocolate into shards.

FRESH JAM DOUGHNUTS

Makes 12

Doughnuts! Not the shop-bought kind, but fresh ones, made at home. This is one of those recipes where you have to remember that all good things take time and patience. It's worth it for the warm, sugary mouthfuls and the sweet smell in the air. I'd never thought about making them myself until a few years ago when my mum came round and I wanted to impress her with something other than a Victoria sponge. She's a hard woman to impress but she ate more than one of these, which was compliment enough. My kids devoured the rest – I can always count on them to make me feel better.

1. Place the flour in a mixing bowl, with the sugar and yeast on one side and the salt on the other. Mix to combine.

2. Put the egg, warm milk and butter into a jug. Make a well in the centre of the dry ingredients and pour in the liquid. If using a stand mixer, attach a dough hook and mix until a dough is formed. If doing it by hand, first bring together using a spatula or the end of a spoon, then get your hands in and combine to make a dough.

3. If you are using a stand mixer, now knead the dough for 5 minutes on high speed. If by hand, grease the work surface and knead for 10 minutes. You will know the dough is ready when it is smooth, shiny and elastic.

4. Grease the inside of a bowl, put the dough in, and cover with cling film. Put in a warm place and leave to double in size. This can take about an hour, sometimes more, sometimes less – it really does depend on the warmth of the room.

5. Once doubled in size, take the dough out and knead for a minute to knock out all the air. Divide into 12 equal pieces and shape into rounds. Place on a greased baking tray and cover with a piece of oiled cling film. Leave for 30 minutes to 1 hour till the dough springs back when you prod with your finger.

6. Put the oil into a pan and heat to 190°C. The oil is hot enough when you drop in a piece of bread and it rises to the top, sizzling.

7. Fry a few doughnuts at a time – don't overcrowd the pan. Cook for 3 minutes on each side, moving them around gently in the oil.

8. Drain on kitchen paper, then, while they're still warm, toss them around in the vanilla sugar. Use a knife to make a small hole in the side into the centre of each one. Carefully pipe in the jam, being careful not to overfill.

PREP 2 HOURS 30 MINUTES
COOKING 25 MINUTES

250g strong bread flour, sifted

40g caster sugar

7g fast-action yeast

1 teaspoon salt

1 medium egg, lightly beaten

150ml warm milk

50g unsalted butter, melted

1½ litres vegetable oil

50g vanilla sugar
(or caster sugar)

350g jam, flavour of
your choice

BAKED CHURROS WITH A SAMOA DIP

Makes 26

I love churros but I try to avoid deep-frying, mostly because it takes at least a day to rid my house of the oily smell. I've even tried blocking the cracks round my doors with tea towels to stop the smell escaping from the kitchen and creeping into other rooms. I will fry if needs must, but I'm always looking for non-fried alternatives like these baked churros. They are very popular in our house, and even more so because of the Samoa dip that accompanies them. Samoas are popular American girl scout cookies of caramel, chocolate and toasted coconut, which I've used as inspiration for this indulgent dip.

PREP 60 MINUTES
COOK 25–30 MINUTES

For the churros

100g unsalted butter, room temperature

250ml water

25g caster sugar

1 teaspoon vanilla extract

125g plain flour, sifted

2 medium eggs, lightly beaten

30g caster sugar, for coating

For the dip

150ml double cream

125g full-fat cream cheese

1 heaped tablespoon ready-made caramel

50g dark chocolate, roughly chopped or grated

20g toasted coconut

1. Preheat the oven to 200°C/180°C fan/gas 6 and cut two large rectangles of baking paper to fit two baking trays.

2. Draw 13 parallel lines, each 8cm long, on each sheet of paper, to use as a guide for piping the churros. Turn the paper over and place one sheet on each baking tray with the pencil lines facing down (make sure you can see them through the paper).

3. Put the butter, water, caster sugar and vanilla extract into a small non-stick pan. Place on a high heat and bring to the boil, then take off the heat immediately.

4. Add the flour and mix really well. The mixture should come together and look something like smooth mash.

5. Slowly add the beaten egg, making sure to whisk all the time. It will look like the mixture is separating, but it isn't. If you persevere it will become a smooth paste. Use up all the egg. Transfer to a bowl and leave to cool for 15 minutes.

6. Attach a large star-tip nozzle to a piping bag. Once the mixture is cool enough to handle, spoon into the piping bag. Using the pencil lines on the paper as a guide, pipe 8cm lines about 2½cm apart, then, using scissors, cut off the ends to get a sharp finish.

7. Bake both trays of churros for 25–30 minutes, until they are crisp and golden. Once baked, leave on the trays for 5 minutes.

8. Spread the sugar on a flat plate, then dip in the churros one by one and set aside.

9. For the dip, whip the cream to soft peaks. Put the cream cheese into a separate bowl and mix till smooth. Add the cream and mix together. Spoon in the caramel and swirl through just enough so you get nice ripples of caramel in the cream.

10. Just before serving, sprinkle the chocolate and golden toasted coconut over the dip.

MALT TIFFIN

— Makes 10–12 slices —

My sister once made tiffin years ago, when we were all just starting out in high school. I remember it was absolutely delicious, and I was so impressed by how few ingredients it involved. Since then, I have enjoyed experimenting with the recipe and adapting it to create new flavour combinations. The recipe never strays from its simplicity but I always find an excuse to incorporate my favourite chocolate treats. This particular tiffin recipe has the distinct flavour of my favourite malt drink, and – even better – it has my favourite chocolate malt balls running through it too!

PREP 30 MINUTES
COOLING 2 HOURS

400g dark chocolate, chopped or chips

200g unsalted butter, diced

4 tablespoons malt extract (or golden syrup)

200g Rich Tea biscuits, crushed fine

1 x 184g bag of chocolate malt balls

3 tablespoons malt powder

1. Line a 23 x 12cm loaf tin with baking paper. If you just line the base and the two longer sides with a strip of paper, this will make it easier to pop the tiffin out when it has set.

2. Put the dark chocolate, butter and malt extract into a heatproof bowl, and place over a pan of water simmering on a low heat till the chocolate and butter have melted. Set aside to cool for a while.

3. I like to crush the biscuits in a food processor, to get fine crumbs. But you can put them into a ziplock bag and use the end of a rolling pin to crush them down if you prefer.

4. Once the chocolate has cooled, add the crushed biscuits and mix until there are no more dry bits of biscuit left.

5. Add the chocolate malt balls whole and give them a thorough mix through. Drop the mixture into the tin and press down firmly to make sure it is well packed. Flatten on top and leave to set in the fridge for at least 2 hours.

6. Take out of the tin before serving. Remove the paper and dust with the malt powder. Cut into slices and serve.

Pudding

I firmly believe that everything in life should end with something sweet. I grew up in a house where we never got dessert after dinner. My dad was an avid eater of fruit. He would wash the microwave plate (because he didn't have another plate big enough) and chop up all the fruit that was really overripe, so he didn't have to throw it away. I'm sure he wanted us to be healthy, but it was also because he had an eye for a bargain, and would buy reduced food even if it was almost rotting. Don't get me wrong: we always had delicious sweet exotic fruits like sharon fruit, physalis, pineapple, mango, jackfruit, all of which do taste better very ripe. But really all we wanted was some pudding. That's probably why we loved school dinners so much. There was nothing nicer than filling your belly with warm Victoria sponge and strawberry custard just before double maths. In this chapter I share the pudding recipes that frequently fill the bellies of the wonderful people in my life – and I know when they eat these they smile from the inside. (Quite a different feeling to having very ripe fruit on your inside!)

ROSEMARY BANOFFEE PIE

Serves 8

A banoffee pie is a delicious thing, but whenever I have made one in the past my brothers and sisters (barring two) have forever complained about it being too sweet. In my head, it's dessert, so it's meant to be sweet. I wanted to stop the moaning, so I decided to create a banoffee pie that was still sweet and delicious and everything it should be, but with a hint of fragrance from rosemary to help balance it. They have since confirmed that they like this version – I won't tell them that I didn't take any of the sugar out!

PREP 20 MINUTES,
PLUS CHILLING
COOK 5 MINUTES

For the base

250g oaty sweet biscuits or digestives, crushed to fine crumbs

100g unsalted butter

For the rosemary caramel

100g unsalted butter

100g molasses sugar

1 x 397g tin of condensed milk

large sprigs of fresh rosemary (approx. 10g), leaves removed and roughly chopped

For the filling

4 small bananas, sliced

300ml double cream

2 tablespoons icing sugar

fresh rosemary leaves, to decorate

1. Grease a 23cm loose-bottomed cake tin and line the base with baking paper.

2. Put the crushed biscuits and the melted butter into a bowl and mix well – the mixture should resemble wet sand.

3. Put the biscuit mixture into the lined tin and use the back of a spoon to press it into the base and around the sides. Be sure to press down firmly to compact the mixture. Put in the fridge to chill for 1 hour.

4. To make the rosemary caramel, put the butter and sugar into a non-stick pan and place on a high heat until the sugar has dissolved, making sure to stir it all the time.

5. Add the condensed milk and bring to the boil, stirring all the time, then turn the heat down and gently simmer for 1–2 minutes, until the mixture has thickened.

6. Take off the heat, beat the caramel for a few seconds with an electric hand whisk to make sure it's smooth, then add the chopped rosemary leaves.

7. Spread the caramel over the base of the tart and place in the fridge for another hour.

8. Whip together the cream and icing sugar, using a hand-held mixer, until the cream has thickened to soft peaks.

9. Place the sliced bananas on top of the caramel, top with the cream and sprinkle with rosemary leaves.

ALMOND & DATE MUFFINS

Makes 12

These muffins are inspired by sticky toffee pudding, one of those desserts that can be steamed slowly and leisurely, which is the best way sometimes. But we live in a time of instant gratification, and much as I love the slow and drawn-out tradition of steamed puds, I am also impatient and often want my ideas to materialize in front of my eyes as fast as possible. These muffins are my solution – they have all the moistness of a sticky date sponge, with a gentle hint of almond, but they are so much faster to put together.

1. Preheat the oven to 180°C/160°C fan/gas 4. Line a 12-hole muffin tin with large paper muffin cases (not cupcake cases, as they aren't tall enough).

2. Put the pitted dates and hot tea into a jug and leave to soak until the tea is completely cold. Then blitz to a smooth paste, using a hand-held mixer.

3. Put the butter and molasses sugar into a bowl and mix until light and fluffy.

4. Add the maple syrup, eggs, almond extract and the blended dates, and mix well, then add the flour and fold through.

5. Divide the mix between the paper cases and bake in the oven for 25–30 minutes, until the muffins have puffed up and a skewer inserted comes out clean.

6. Leave in the tin for 10 minutes, then take out the muffins and leave to cool on a wire rack.

7. To make the maple cream frosting, put the butter, icing sugar, milk and maple syrup into a bowl and whisk until light and fluffy. Pipe the mixture on top of the cooled muffins.

8. Divide the marzipan into 12 small pieces and roll them into sausage shapes. Stuff each date with a piece of marzipan and top each muffin with a date.

PREP 40 MINUTES
COOK 30 MINUTES

For the muffins
200g pitted dates

250ml hot tea

125g unsalted butter, softened

200g molasses sugar

2 tablespoons maple syrup

3 medium eggs

2 teaspoons almond extract

250g self-raising flour, sifted

For the maple cream
200g unsalted butter, softened

400g icing sugar, sifted

2 tablespoons whole milk

2 tablespoons maple syrup

For the decoration
25g golden marzipan

12 dates, pitted

LEMON & BLACK CHIA DRIZZLE LOAF

Serves 8–10

This lemon drizzle loaf is a simple cake by anyone's standards. Lemon is often paired with poppy seeds, and while I agree that it's a great combination, here I've decided to change it up a little and use black chia seeds instead. They still add that little extra crunch and colour, plus they also provide extra fibre, for anyone who worries about that sort of thing when it comes to cake!

PREP 25 MINUTES
COOK 1 HOUR

For the loaf
225g unsalted butter, softened

225g caster sugar

4 medium eggs

zest of 2 lemons (reserve juice for later)

50g black chia seeds

225g self-raising flour, sifted

2 tablespoons whole milk

For the drizzle
juice of the 2 lemons above

150g caster sugar

1. Preheat the oven to 180°C/160°C fan/gas 4. Grease an 8 x 21cm rectangular loaf tin (a 900g loaf tin) and line it with baking paper.

2. Using a stand or hand-held mixer, put the butter into a bowl with the sugar and beat until light and fluffy.

3. Add the eggs one at a time, making sure to mix well after each addition. Stir in the lemon zest.

4. Add the chia seeds to the sifted flour. Mix to distribute the seeds.

5. Fold the dry mix into the wet mix, using a spatula, adding the milk to help loosen the mixture.

6. Pour the batter into the lined tin and bake for 55 minutes–1 hour, until the cake is golden, risen, and a skewer inserted comes out clean.

7. Take the cake out of the oven and set aside, still in the tin.

8. To make the drizzle, mix together the lemon juice and sugar. Pour the drizzle all over the cake, then leave to cool completely in the tin.

SWEET SCONES WITH COCONUT CREAM & PINK PEPPERCORN PINEAPPLE JAM

Makes 9

There are many arguments had about scones. Are they from Cornwall or Devon? What goes on first, cream or jam? Butter or no butter? To sandwich or not? But I think all these arguments are irrelevant. When you love a scone, who cares how you eat it? To prove my point, here I've gone for something completely different, a total reinvention of the classic, with whipped coconut cream instead of clotted cream and fragrant pineapple jam instead of strawberry.

1. Start by making the jam. Put the pineapple, sugar, lime leaves and peppercorns into a pan, set on a high heat and bring to the boil, then reduce to a medium heat and let the mixture bubble.

2. You need the jam mixture to reach 105°C – this should take about 4 minutes and you can test it with a sugar thermometer. If you don't have one, instead place a plate in the freezer in advance. Place a drop of the jam on the cold plate and leave for a few seconds. Push it with your finger and if it wrinkles the jam is ready. Keep testing this way until you have visible wrinkles. Transfer the jam to a bowl to cool completely.

3. Preheat the oven to 220°C/200°C fan/gas 7 and line a baking tray with baking paper.

4. Put the flour, sugar, baking powder and salt into a large bowl, and mix roughly. Now add the butter and rub it in using your fingertips until the mixture resembles breadcrumbs.

5. Make a well in the centre and add the milk. Mix with a palette knife, then get your hands in and gently bring the dough together.

6. Turn the dough out on to a lightly dusted surface and roll out to a 15 x 15cm square. Then cut into 9 squares, 5 x 5cm. Place on the baking tray, brush the tops with milk and bake on the middle shelf for 12–15 minutes.

7. While the scones are baking, make the coconut cream. Scoop up the solidified cream at the top of the tin, getting rid of the liquid underneath, then whip the cream using a whisk. Add the vanilla bean paste and icing sugar – it won't change too much in consistency but will just be fluffier and easier to spoon. Leave in the fridge, covered, while you wait for the scones.

8. Take the scones out of the oven and leave to cool completely on a wire rack. Split and enjoy with cream and jam, or jam and cream, in whichever order you prefer.

PREP 40 MINUTES,
PLUS COOLING
COOK 25 MINUTES

For the jam

1 x 435g tin of crushed pineapple (280g drained weight)

280g jam sugar

9 dried kaffir lime leaves, crushed

2 teaspoons pink peppercorns, crushed

For the scones

350g self-raising flour, plus extra for dusting

3 tablespoons caster sugar

½ teaspoon baking powder

½ teaspoon salt

85g unsalted butter, cubed

185ml whole milk, plus extra for glazing

For the coconut cream

1 x 400g tin of coconut cream, from the fridge

1 teaspoon vanilla bean paste

1 tablespoon icing sugar

CARDAMOM RICE PUDDING BRÛLÉES WITH MANGO, COCONUT & LIME

Serves 8

Lots of people seem to have bad memories of tepid rice pudding, full of huge uncooked grains of rice and with a dollop of cold jam in the middle. Well, that was my school dinner through and through, and that's how I thought rice pudding was meant to be. Until I tried the tinned stuff and then I thought, ah, that's how it's meant to be. Until I ate my little brother's jar of baby rice and thought maybe that's what it was meant to taste like. Until I discovered a third way. My sister and I were at a wedding where they served these delicious tiny cold pots of rice pudding, and after devouring our own we set off around the room to see who might want help with theirs. With those pots in mind, I created this recipe. It's a smoother rice pudding with a delicate hint of cardamom, set until cold, then topped with sugar and blowtorched for a crisp caramel top. If you don't like rice pudding, this might change your mind.

PREP 15 MINUTES, PLUS SOAKING AND CHILLING COOK 25 MINUTES

For the rice pudding

100g basmati rice

400ml cold water

600ml double cream

5 green cardamom pods, crushed, husks removed and seeds ground

100g caster sugar, plus 60g for the brûlée

For the mango, coconut and lime

2 large mangoes (approx. 500g), peeled and cut into small chunks

zest and juice of 1 lime

25g toasted coconut chips

1. Soak the rice in the water for 1 hour. Transfer the water and rice to a jug, then, using a stick blender, blitz until the rice is ground to tiny pieces.

2. Put the rice and water mixture into a non-stick pan and turn the heat up to high. Add the cream and the ground cardamom seeds and bring to the boil, stirring continuously over a medium heat until thickened. This should take only 15–20 minutes.

3. Take off the heat and leave to cool for 15 minutes, then stir in the sugar.

4. Divide the pudding between eight 150ml ramekins and flatten the tops, using the back of a spoon. Put the ramekins on a tray and chill for an hour.

5. Before serving, sprinkle 1½ teaspoons of sugar on the top of each ramekin, spreading it out with the back of a spoon to make an even layer.

6. Brûlée using a blowtorch (make sure the ramekins are on a heat-resistant surface) until the top is golden brown and bubbling.

7. Mix the chopped mango with the lime zest and juice, then stir in the coconut chips. Serve with the rice pudding brûlées.

Tip: If you don't have a blowtorch you can place the ramekins under a grill to caramelise the tops, but be sure to watch them all the time.

CHAI TEA BANANA CAKE

Serves 8–12

Banana in cake is for me the best way to use up very ripe and unappealing bananas sitting in a bowl full of otherwise crisp fresh fruit. The moisture with which the banana permeates the cake is like no other. Here I've paired it with flavours of a traditional Indian chai, and have also added another element of moisture, in the form of a vanilla-flavoured cheesecake topping, to mimic the beautiful creamy milky froth on top of a cup of chai.

PREP 25 MINUTES
COOK 55 MINUTES–1 HOUR

For the cake

200g unsalted butter, softened

200g light brown sugar

4 medium eggs

2 ripe bananas, mashed

200g self-raising flour, sifted

1 teaspoon ground cinnamon

1 teaspoon ground cardamom (or ground seeds from about 20 pods)

1 teaspoon ground ginger

½ teaspoon baking powder

For the topping

150g mascarpone

1 medium egg yolk

1 teaspoon vanilla bean paste

1 tablespoon caster sugar

1 tablespoon plain flour

1 tablespoon icing sugar for dusting

1. Preheat the oven to 180°C/160°C fan/gas 4. Grease the base and sides of a deep 20cm cake tin and line with baking paper so that the paper comes a couple of centimetres above the side of the tin.

2. Put the butter and sugar into a large bowl and beat for 5 minutes, until light and fluffy.

3. Add the eggs one at a time, mixing after each addition.

4. Add the bananas and lightly mix together to incorporate, then add the sifted flour, cinnamon, cardamom, ginger and baking powder, and mix well.

5. Put the mixture into the prepared cake tin, levelling off the top.

6. Put the mascarpone, egg yolk, vanilla, sugar and flour into a small bowl and mix well until everything is incorporated. Don't beat it for too long, as it can become runny.

7. Make 5 hollows in the top of the cake mixture and spoon the mixture into them.

8. Now bake in the oven for 50 minutes–1 hour, covering the top with foil after 30 minutes to prevent the cheesecake topping taking on too much colour. You will know the cake is baked when a skewer inserted comes out clean.

9. Leave to cool in the tin for 20 minutes, then take out of the tin and finish cooling on a rack. When cool, dust with icing sugar.

FLAPJACK CINNAMON APPLE CRUMBLE WITH VANILLA CUSTARD

Serves 6

Most of my dessert memories involve a stainless steel kitchen and large silver trays of steaming goodies in a very cold school canteen. Never too sure about stewed fruit, when I first saw apple crumble in those trays, I prepared myself for the worst. But it was delicious! I always prayed not to get the custard skin that formed under the heat lamps. If I did, it was a straight swap with my best friend, who loved it. Apple crumble is now a go-to in our house. I've added a few spices and abandoned the powdered custard, but it's still as heart- and belly-warming as it was back then. I'm just grateful I don't have PE straight after.

1. Preheat the oven to 150°C/130°C fan/gas 2. Spread the oats on a large baking tray and toast in the oven for 10–15 minutes, stirring once, until they are golden in colour.

2. Once toasted, put the oats into a bowl and add the lemon zest. Leave the oven on.

3. Put the butter, sugar and syrup in a pan and place on a medium heat until the butter has melted and the sugar has dissolved. Pour over the oats in the bowl, give it a good mix and set aside.

4. Peel and core the apples and cut into chunks. Put the prepared apples, butter, cinnamon, 1 tablespoon of sugar and the lemon juice into a pan. Cook for about 10 minutes on a medium heat, until the apples have softened slightly.

5. Stir in the cornflour and raisins, then taste for sweetness and add the other 1 tablespoon of sugar if you like. Tip into a 25cm square or round baking dish. Cover the apples with the oat mixture.

6. Bake on the middle shelf of the oven for 40–45 minutes.

7. Meanwhile, make the custard. Put the milk and vanilla into a pan and bring to the boil, then leave on a simmer.

8. Put the egg yolks, sugar and cornflour into a separate bowl and whisk with a balloon whisk until the mixture is light. Slowly add the warm milk in a steady stream, making sure to whisk all the time. Once all the milk is added, pour it all back into the pan and stir gently with a spoon till the mixture thickens.

9. Pour straight into a serving jug and, if there is a wait, cover with cling film, making sure the film touches the top of the custard (unless you like a skin, in which case by all means leave it exposed). Serve the crumble with the custard alongside.

PREP 40 MINUTES
COOK 1 HOUR 35 MINUTES

For the flapjack crumble
250g porridge oats

2 teaspoons lemon zest

125g unsalted butter

100g muscovado sugar

100g golden syrup

For the apples
1kg Granny Smith or cooking apples

40g unsalted butter

1 teaspoon cinnamon

1–2 tablespoons muscovado sugar

juice of 1 lemon

1 tablespoon cornflour

150g raisins

For the vanilla custard
600ml whole milk

1 tablespoon vanilla bean extract

4 egg yolks

20g caster sugar

2 teaspoons cornflour

Pudding 219

MANGO & PASSION FRUIT
JAM ROLY-POLY

Serves 6–8

I don't remember ever eating a jam roly-poly as a child, but my husband does. So when he told me, 'I used to eat jam roly-poly at school,' that for me was a challenge right there! Why have any old jam roly-poly when you can have a mango and passion fruit one? This is a steamed pudding the old-fashioned way, but with a modern tropical twist. The jam recipe here makes about 500g and only about a third of it is needed for the roly-poly but it's tricky to make in much smaller quantities. The good news is that it keeps really well in a jar in the fridge, so you'll have some left over for another time.

1. For the jam, put the mango, passion fruit pulp and sugar into a pan and stir to combine, then bring the mixture to the boil.

2. Bring the mixture to 105°C, then take off the heat and place in a bowl to cool completely.

3. Meanwhile, preheat the oven to 180°C/160°C fan/gas 4 and place a deep roasting dish in the bottom, making sure there is a shelf directly above it. Place a large sheet of foil on your work surface. Place a large sheet of greaseproof paper on top of it, the same size, and grease the top of the paper all over.

4. Put the flour into a bowl with the butter and suet and rub with your fingertips until the mixture resembles breadcrumbs. Make a well in the centre and add the milk, then bring the dough together.

5. Roll out the dough on a floured surface to a square roughly 30 x 30cm. Spread about 150g of the jam all over the square, leaving just the edges bare. (Store the remaining jam in a jar in the fridge to use for something else.)

6. Roll up the dough like a Swiss roll, and seal the long seam and the edges tightly. Place on the buttered paper, seam-side down.

7. Wrap the roll in the paper and foil loosely, as it will expand in the oven. Seal the edges, then place directly on the oven shelf and bake for 1 hour.

8. Leave in the wrapping for 10 minutes after baking, then unravel, slice and serve. We like to eat this hot out of the oven with cold ice cream, or, if we're being nostalgic for my husband's sake, we have it with custard.

Photos overleaf →

PREP 45 MINUTES
COOK 1 HOUR

For the jam

220g mango, finely chopped

80g passion fruit pulp (this is the pulp of 3 passion fruit) – all in all you want to make up 300g of fruit combined

300g jam sugar

For the suet pastry

250g self-raising flour, plus extra for dusting

50g unsalted butter, plus extra for greasing

50g vegetable suet

150ml whole milk

BUTTERSCOTCH BISCUIT BLONDIES

Makes 16

A blondie is not an homage to an 80s singer, it's the opposite of a brownie. By which I mean it's essentially a brownie recipe, but turns out a pale golden colour, rather than dark brown. These ones include pecans and butterscotch chips, plus a bonus layer of biscuit in the base that gives the old blondie a little something extra to scream and shout about.

1. Preheat the oven to 190°C/170°C fan/gas 5. Line the base and sides of a rectangular cake tin, 30 x 23cm, with baking paper.

2. Place the crushed biscuits in a bowl with the melted butter and mix till there is no more dry biscuit.

3. Put the mixture into the prepared tin, then, using the palms of your hands, push the biscuit mix down so it is compact.

4. Bake in the oven for 20 minutes, then take out and leave to cool while you prepare the blondie top.

5. Put the butter, sugar, eggs, flour, butterscotch chips and pecans into a bowl and mix together for 2 minutes, until well combined.

6. Spoon the mixture on top of the baked biscuit base and put back into the oven for 30 minutes, then take out and leave to cool for 30 minutes in the tin.

7. Cut into chunks and serve.

PREP 25 MINUTES
COOK 50 MINUTES

For the base
500g malted milk biscuits, crushed

200g unsalted butter, melted

For the blondie top
225g unsalted butter, softened

225g caster sugar

4 medium eggs

150g plain flour

200g butterscotch chips

100g pecans, roughly chopped

STRAWBERRY & MINT BAKED CHEESECAKE

Serves 8–12

I'm sure we've all sat at a dinner table and discussed which is better: baked cheesecake or the non-baked kind. No? Well, I have had that discussion even if you haven't, and the realization that all my diners unanimously preferred a baked cheesecake came just as I was a breath away from presenting the 'other' kind! I'm happy to say the cheesecake was consumed all the same, of course, but the incident made me sit up in bed scouring books for recipes. Not an unfamiliar scene in my bed. Since then, I've come to absolutely love the gentle nature of baking a cheesecake. It's slow but the results are velvety smooth and worth the wait. This baked cheesecake is topped with a deliciously fragrant strawberry and mint compote.

**PREP 30 MINUTES,
PLUS CHILLING
COOK 1 HOUR 30 MINUTES**

For the base

150g digestive biscuits,
crushed to fine crumbs

75g unsalted butter, melted

For the filling

900g full-fat cream cheese

200g caster sugar

200ml double cream

3 tablespoons plain flour

3 eggs

1 egg yolk

2 tablespoons vanilla
bean paste

For the compote

400g strawberries,
hulled and quartered

80g caster sugar

1½ tablespoons lemon juice

a large handful of fresh mint
(approx. 10g), finely chopped

1. Grease the base of a 23cm loose-bottomed cake tin, making sure to secure the base (trust me, you don't want to go there!). Make sure to grease the sides well too. Line the base of the tin with baking paper.

2. Preheat the oven to 200°C/180°C fan/gas 6.

3. Put the crushed biscuits and melted butter into a bowl and mix until the mixture resembles wet sand and there are no dry clumps remaining.

4. Put the mixture into the cake tin and use the palms of your hands to push it down until it is all compact and tight in the base.

5. Bake on the middle shelf for 10 minutes, then remove and set aside to cool. Reduce the oven to 160°C/140°C fan/gas 3.

6. Put the cream cheese, caster sugar and double cream into a large bowl. Mix to soften the mixture so it's all viscous.

7. Now add the flour, eggs, egg yolk and vanilla paste and mix again, to get a smooth, even batter.

8. Put the kettle on to boil. Wrap the outside of the cake tin with two layers of foil to make sure it's completely watertight, then place the tin in a large roasting dish and fill the dish with boiling water to come halfway up the outside of the cake tin.

9. Pour in the cheesecake mixture on top of the biscuit base, then cover the roasting tin with a large tent of foil, securing it around the edges of the tin – this will keep the steam in as the cheesecake bakes.

10. Bake the cheesecake for 1 hour. You will know it is ready when it's golden and firm around the edge but still has a slight wobble in the centre. If it's still very wobbly, bake for another 10–15 minutes, checking it often.

11. Once the cheesecake is baked, turn off the oven, open the oven door wide and leave the cheesecake in there for 2 hours. It will become firmer as it cools.

12. After 2 hours, take the cheesecake out of the oven and out of the roasting tin and put it into the fridge overnight.

13. To prepare the compote, put the strawberries into a pan with the sugar and lemon juice. Cook for about 10–12 minutes on a medium heat, until the sugar has melted and the sauce has reduced slightly. Transfer the mixture to a bowl and leave to cool completely, then stir in the fresh mint.

14. Take the cheesecake out of the fridge, transfer to a serving plate or stand, and top with the strawberry and mint compote.

ORANGE SCENTED POLENTA CAKE WITH ROSEMARY, THYME & PISTACHIOS

Serves 6-8

Polenta is an Italian maize flour that works brilliantly in cakes. It has quite a unique texture but not much in the way of its own flavour, which means it can carry other tastes and flavours really well, especially citrus. When baked in a cake, it produces a sturdy structure and acts like a hidden sponge, drawing in all the delicious flavour from the thyme and orange syrup that it gets drizzled with here. The shiny, nutty, floral icing is a pretty finishing touch.

PREP 25 MINUTES
COOK 1 HOUR

For the cake

180ml mild olive oil

220g caster sugar

300g ground almonds

3 large eggs

zest of 4 mandarins (save juice for the syrup, see below)

1 tablespoon fresh rosemary leaves, finely chopped

1 tablespoon orange blossom water

150g ground polenta

1 teaspoon baking powder

For the syrup and icing

juice of 4 mandarins

4 tablespoons runny orange blossom honey

5 sprigs of fresh lemon thyme

50g icing sugar, sifted

100-120ml pistachio or walnut oil

1 teaspoon orange blossom water

25g pistachio nibs or peeled pistachios, for decoration

1. Preheat the oven to 200°C/180°C fan/gas 6. Grease a 20cm round cake tin and line the base and sides with baking paper.

2. Whisk the olive oil and sugar together, using an electric beater, for about 5 minutes, until well combined.

3. Add a little of the ground almonds and mix well. Add 1 egg and mix well. Then add a little more ground almonds, mix, and repeat, adding an egg and more ground almonds until both are used up.

4. Mix in the mandarin zest, rosemary and orange blossom water.

5. In a separate bowl, mix together the polenta and baking powder. Add to the wet ingredients and fold through until everything is incorporated well.

6. Spoon the batter into the prepared tin, spread to the edges and level off the top. Bake on the middle shelf of the oven for 30 minutes, then turn the heat down to 180°C/160°C fan/gas 4 and bake for a further 25-30 minutes. The cake should be a deep golden brown and a skewer inserted should come out clean.

7. Meanwhile, for the syrup, put the mandarin juice, honey and thyme sprigs into a pan and warm through gently so that the honey and juice mix together - don't let the mixture boil. Take off the heat and set aside, leaving the thyme sprigs to infuse until you are ready to use the syrup.

8. When the cake is ready, take it out of the oven and poke holes all over it, using a skewer. Leave to cool for 5 minutes. Drizzle all the syrup (remove the thyme sprigs) over the cake while it is still warm. Leave in the tin for about 30 minutes, to cool almost completely, then remove from the tin.

9. Meanwhile, mix together the icing sugar, pistachio oil and orange blossom water with a small whisk until you reach a drizzling consistency. Drizzle over the cooled cake and sprinkle with the pistachio nibs.

PEANUT BUTTER CHOCOLATE STACK

Serves 10

My husband Abdal and I ate something very full of peanut butter a long time ago and he has been asking me to make something similar for a while. Did I give him what he wanted? Of course, even though I had a million other things to bake and a million other ideas to create. But writing the recipes for this chapter seemed like the perfect opportunity to satisfy his peanut butter needs.

PREP 45 MINUTES

COOK 20 MINUTES

For the cake
6 medium eggs

170g caster sugar

170g plain flour

40g cocoa powder

1 teaspoon baking powder

For the ganache
200g dark chocolate chips
(70% cocoa solids)

200ml double cream

For the caramel
100g butter

100g light brown sugar

1 x 397g tin of condensed milk

1 teaspoon salt

150ml double cream

To assemble
300g crunchy peanut butter

2 tablespoons cocoa powder

1. Preheat the oven to 200°C/180°C fan/gas 6. Grease the base and sides of two 23 x 33cm Swiss roll tins. Line with baking paper.

2. Put the eggs and sugar into the bowl of a mixer and beat for about 8 minutes till lighter in colour and tripled in volume. Lift the beaters and swirl the mixture in a figure of 8 – if the shape remains on the surface for more than 8 seconds, the eggs are ready.

3. Sift together the flour, cocoa powder and baking powder, then fold into the egg mix using a metal spoon, making sure not to lose all the air you worked so hard to create. When no more flour particles can be seen, divide the mixture between the two tins, easing it into the corners.

4. Bake the cakes for 10 minutes. Once ready, turn them out of the tins, using the paper to help, and leave to cool on a wire rack.

5. To make the ganache, put the chocolate chips into a bowl. Bring the cream to the boil in a small pan, pour it over the chocolate and give it a stir. Allow the heat of the cream to gently melt the chocolate. Stir again after 5 minutes and you should have a glossy smooth ganache. Set aside to cool.

6. To make the caramel, put the butter and sugar into a pan on a medium heat. Once the sugar has melted, add the condensed milk and turn the heat up to high, making sure to stir all the time.

7. Bring the mixture to the boil, then cook for 2 minutes on a high heat. Take off the heat, stir in the salt and cream, and set aside to cool. Once the mixture has thickened to a spreading consistency, transfer to a bowl to cool.

8. Ensure all the components are completely cool before starting to assemble. Peel the paper off the cakes and cut them both down the middle vertically, to get 4 long thin rectangles. Spread the first slice with peanut butter, then with ganache. Chill for a few minutes before adding a layer of caramel.

9. Top with the next layer of cake and repeat the fillings, till you have three layers of filling and the fourth layer of cake is on top. Dust the cake with cocoa powder and cut into long thin slices.

ROSE, RASPBERRY & COCONUT FOOL

Makes 6 x 150ml pots

I always seem to have cream and fruit in the fridge, just two of the many ingredients I tend to buy too much of and never learn my lesson about. What better way to use them up than to make a fool – not out of you or me, but out of the ingredients! (Unless of course you over-whip the cream, and then who's the fool?) This simple dessert involves deliciously stewed raspberries rippled through a sweet rose-flavoured cream and topped with toasted coconut.

PREP 15 MINUTES
COOK 15 MINUTES

450g raspberries, plus an extra 150g for the top

50g caster sugar

a squeeze of lemon juice

300ml double cream

5 tablespoons caster sugar

100ml Greek yoghurt

2–3 tablespoons rose water

30–50g toasted coconut flakes

a small handful of crystallized rose petals

1. Put the raspberries and 50g of sugar into a pan and add the lemon juice. Press the berries lightly with the back of a fork, but be sure not to break them down completely. You want a few chunks of fruit. Cook on a medium heat for 10–15 minutes, until the mixture thickens, then take off the heat and set aside to cool completely.

2. Meanwhile, put the cream into a bowl with the 5 tablespoons of sugar and whip to soft peaks. Add the yoghurt and rose water and whip again gently.

3. Pour in the cooled raspberry mixture and ripple through, using the back of a knife.

4. Spoon the mixture into six 150ml pots and leave to chill in the fridge for at least an hour.

5. Before serving, top with some extra raspberries, toasted coconut flakes and crystallized rose petals.

MINT CHOCOLATE CHIP
ICE CREAM SANDWICHES

Serves 6

What's better than a cookie? Two cookies, of course! But what's better than two cookies? Well, two cookies with ice cream in between! I think that's enough said – shall we continue?

PREP 30 MINUTES,
PLUS FREEZING
COOK 20 MINUTES

For the cookies

170g unsalted butter, softened

300g light brown sugar

1 medium egg

1 egg yolk

200g plain flour, sifted

50g cocoa powder, sifted

a pinch of salt

½ teaspoon baking powder

100g dark chocolate, chopped
or chips

For the chocolate
chip ice cream

900ml vanilla ice cream
(450g in weight)

2 teaspoons peppermint
extract

a few drops of green
food colouring

100g milk chocolate chips

1. Preheat the oven to 180°C/160°C fan/gas 4. Line two baking trays with baking paper.

2. Put the butter and sugar into the bowl of a mixer and beat until the mixture is almost white. Add the egg and egg yolk and mix well.

3. Put the flour, cocoa powder, salt and baking powder into a bowl and whisk together so they are well combined.

4. Add the wet mix to the dry mix, along with the dark chocolate chips, and mix to combine. The mixture will be quite stiff.

5. Divide into 12 equal mounds (about 65g each) on the lined baking trays, leaving a space between them of about 5cm, so they have room to spread. Try to keep the mounds the same shape, so they are easy to pair up when sandwiching.

6. Bake in the oven for 18–20 minutes. Once baked, leave on the tray to cool completely.

7. Meanwhile, take out the ice cream and allow it to soften just very slightly. Transfer it to a bowl and add the peppermint extract, green food colouring and chocolate chips. Mix till all the ice cream is green. This is easiest with an electric hand whisk, if you have one, otherwise do it by hand.

8. Put the ice cream back into the freezer, ideally in a shallow container, and leave for 30 minutes or until it has set again.

9. Sort the chocolate cookies into pairs. Divide the ice cream between 6 of the cookies and sandwich together with the other 6.

10. Squeeze the cookies so as to distribute the ice cream evenly, and eat.

RHUBARB & CUSTARD
ICE CREAM SANDWICHES
——— *Serves 4 (makes about 850ml ice cream)* ———

My family often profess their love for ice cream, and much as I love making a proper churned version from scratch, I also enjoy an easy way out. This ice cream recipe is the easy type: a simple no-churn variety, rippled with tangy rhubarb compote, then sandwiched between two crisp custardy biscuits.

1. Put the rhubarb, sugar, lime juice and glucose into a small non-stick pan and cook gently for 10–12 minutes, until the rhubarb has softened and broken down. Take off the heat and transfer to another bowl. Add the rhubarb essence, stir and leave to cool completely.

2. Meanwhile, make the ice cream by combining the condensed milk, cream, vanilla and glucose. Whisk the mixture until it forms soft peaks.

3. Add the cooled rhubarb mixture and fold through to create a ripple effect. Transfer to a container with a lid, place the container in a ziplock bag and freeze for at least 4 hours.

4. Meanwhile, get started on the biscuits. Put the butter and sugar into a bowl. Mix together, then add the egg and the almond extract and mix again. Add the flour and custard powder and mix to form a dough. Flatten the dough, wrap in cling film, and leave to chill for an hour.

5. Preheat the oven to 190°C/170°C fan/gas 5 and line a baking tray with baking paper.

6. Unwrap the dough and roll out on a floured work surface to ¾cm thick. Using a 6.5cm round straight-edged cutter, cut out circles. Collect the offcuts, roll again and cut out more circles until you have used all the dough. You should have 8 biscuits, to make 4 sandwiches.

7. Place them on the baking tray, prick them with a fork to stop them rising too much, and bake for 20–22 minutes until lightly golden but visibly yellow from the custard powder.

8. Leave to cool completely on the tray. Once cool, take large scoops of ice cream and sandwich each scoop between 2 biscuits.

PREP 25 MINUTES, PLUS
CHILLING AND FREEZING
COOK 35 MINUTES

For the rhubarb compote

100g rhubarb, cut into
2.5cm pieces

20g caster sugar

juice of ½ a lime

1 teaspoon liquid glucose

5 drops of rhubarb essence

For the ice cream

½ x 397g tin of sweetened
condensed milk

300ml double cream

1 teaspoon vanilla extract

2 teaspoons liquid glucose

For the custard biscuits

75g unsalted butter, softened

75g caster sugar

1 medium egg, lightly beaten

½ teaspoon almond extract

100g plain flour, sifted, plus
extra for dusting

75g custard powder

SUMMER FRUIT SEMIFREDDO

Serves 6

This is my take on a summer pudding. I like to use frozen berries that I've got stashed away from pick-your-own summer afternoons with the kids. This is a perfect way of using them up. Like a classic summer pudding, I soak the bread, but instead of filling it with just fruit, my version is filled with fruit and also a quick and easy semifreddo. It's not only delicious to eat but really beautiful to cut into.

PREP 45 MINUTES

FREEZE 3 HOURS

400g frozen mixed summer fruits

100g caster sugar

3 tablespoons water

7 slices of white bread (about 170g), crusts removed, halved lengthways

600ml double cream

2 tablespoons golden syrup

1. Put the frozen fruit, sugar and water into a medium pan and bring to the boil, then take off the heat. You don't want the fruit to break down too much but you want to extract as much liquid as possible.

2. Drain the fruit through a sieve, making sure to catch all the liquid in a bowl. Use the back of a spoon to push through as much liquid as possible. Then leave the liquid to cool completely.

3. Line a 20cm round Pyrex dish with cling film.

4. Dip each piece of bread quickly into the fruit juice mixture and place around the edge of the dish vertically, slightly overlapping each piece with the next to prevent leaking. Do this all around the edges – you should have one piece left. Break that piece down to size, then dip it in the fruit juice and place it in the base of the dish. Set aside.

5. Whip the double cream to soft peaks, then add the golden syrup and mix well. Add the fruit and just ripple through gently.

6. Put the cream mixture into the lined bowl and spread it level on top. If any of the bread pieces come up higher than the top of the cream, simply fold them over. Cover the top with cling film and place in the freezer for 3 hours.

7. To turn out, tip on to a plate and remove all the cling film. Cut into wedges and serve.

APPLE, FIG, BRIE & HONEY STRUDEL

Serves 6–8

My brother-in-law's favourite dessert in the whole wide world is strudel, which he usually buys frozen from the supermarket freezer aisle. While there is absolutely nothing wrong with ready-made desserts, I enjoy making him my own versions to see if I can create one that he likes even better. Granted, I don't make the pastry in this recipe, but I'm also a firm believer that there is absolutely nothing wrong with a bit of shop-bought pastry – it's how you plait it here that really makes the difference.

1. Preheat the oven to 220°C/200°C fan/gas 7 and place a baking tray in the oven.

2. The pastry should come rolled, with baking paper already around it. Unravel the pastry and lay it on the work surface, on its paper.

3. Make two light scoring marks along the pastry to divide the piece lengthways into three equal strips (don't actually cut through, as you need it all to stay joined together), then make a mark 5cm in from both ends of each score mark. Cut from the 5cm mark as shown overleaf, to remove a small section of pastry from each corner, which will leave a small central rectangular flap at each end.

4. Starting from the 5cm mark, make parallel angled cuts in the two outside strips of pastry, 2.5cm apart, leaving the central strip untouched and ready to fill.

5. Chill the prepared pastry in the fridge for 15 minutes.

6. Lay the apple on top of the chilled pastry base, down the central strip. Now add the figs, followed by the Brie. Drizzle the honey all over.

7. Fold over the rectangular flap of pastry at one end. Then alternate the pastry strips over the filling until you reach the end, and finish by folding over the second rectangular flap.

8. Brush the pastry with beaten egg and sprinkle with the sugar.

9. Take the hot baking tray out of the oven and place the pastry, still on its baking paper, on the tray. Bake for 25–30 minutes.

10. Remove from the oven and leave to cool on the tray. Dust with a little icing sugar to finish.

PREP 40 MINUTES
COOK 30 MINUTES

1 x 320g pack of ready-rolled puff pastry

1 green apple (approx. 90g), cored and thinly sliced

2 figs (or 4 if small) (approx. 80g), thinly sliced

90g Brie, sliced

30ml honey

1 egg, lightly beaten

2 tablespoons demerara sugar

1 tablespoon icing sugar

Something Special

The puddings in the previous chapter are for everyday eating, to end any meal. But when it comes to special occasions, there's something wonderful about giving up your time to create a showstopping dessert or cake that is that both beautiful and delicious. No present can really compare to that moment when you walk into the room with something a little bit special, be it frosted, coated, towering, piled with decorations or sparkling with glitter. It's the kind of gift that instantly says, 'I love you.' So this is a collection of some of my favourite sweet bakes, desserts and treats that will instantly show your guests and loved ones that you went out of your way to make an effort.

TIRAMISÙ CAKE

— Serves 8 —

My hot drink of choice has always been a good cup of Yorkshire tea, lightly brewed with a splash of milk. It's my favourite treat first thing in the morning, and as soon as the babies have settled into bed. Cuppa, cuddles and the comfort of my sofa. Unless of course Abdal sits down next to me with a cup of his strong-brewed coffee, hot out of his special coffee machine. The smell of strong coffee makes my stomach turn, and has done since my third pregnancy, but strangely enough I can just about bear the pain if I know it's about to be mixed into cake, or tiramisù. Or – best of all – tiramisù cake. Need I say more?

PREP 45 MINUTES, PLUS COOLING AND CHILLING
COOK 35 MINUTES

For the cake

225g unsalted butter, softened, plus extra for greasing

240g sponge fingers (approx. 36)

60ml whole milk

3 tablespoons instant coffee

225g light brown sugar

4 medium eggs

225g self-raising flour, sifted

1 teaspoon baking powder

100ml boiling water

4 tablespoons instant coffee

3 tablespoons cocoa powder

For the vanilla mascarpone cream

300ml double cream

50g caster sugar

250g full-fat mascarpone cheese

1 tablespoon vanilla bean paste

1. Preheat the oven to 180°C/160°C fan/gas 4. Grease the base of two 20cm round springform cake tins and line with baking paper.

2. Line the base of each tin with the sponge fingers, sugary side facing down. As you line, make sure to cut, carve and get the fingers to the right length to fit all the gaps in the base. If the fingers are tightly packed this will stop them rising to the top while baking. So take your time, making sure you fill as many of the gaps as possible.

3. Once you have done this, set aside and get started on the coffee mixture. Put the milk and coffee into a small pan and warm just until the coffee has dissolved into the milk. Leave the mixture to one side to cool completely.

4. Put the butter and sugar into the bowl of a mixer, or use an electric hand-held mixer, and beat until it is light, fluffy and almost white in colour. This can take 10 minutes on a medium to high speed. You can also mix by hand, but it will take a bit longer.

5. Add the eggs one at a time, making sure to incorporate them well, then add the flour and baking powder and fold through until well combined. Add the coffee mixture and fold that in too.

6. Divide the mixture between the two tins and spread it all over the sponge fingers that you've laid down so precisely. Level off the top and bake for 30–35 minutes, until a skewer inserted comes out clean.

7. When the cakes are baked you will find that they don't have a smooth surface like a normal cake does. Instead, there will be small bubbles all over the surface. This is just the air from the sponge fingers and is nothing to worry about. You may even have a rogue sponge finger that has come to the top, but that doesn't matter too much.

Recipe continues overleaf →

8. Leave the cakes to cool in the tins, then turn out on to a wire rack to cool completely, sponge finger side up.

9. When the cakes are completely cool, put the boiling water and the coffee into a small jug or bowl and stir to dissolve. Brush the tops of the cakes (the sides with the sponge fingers exposed) with the hot coffee mixture. Be sure to use up all of the liquid.

10. Make the vanilla mascarpone cream just before assembling. Put the cream and sugar into a bowl and whisk until it has just thickened very slightly.

11. Now put the mascarpone and vanilla bean paste into another bowl and whisk to loosen the mascarpone. This way it will incorporate better with the cream.

12. Fold the cream into the mascarpone.

13. Take one of the springform tins you baked the cake in and grease the inside again. Line generously with cling film, making sure there is an overhang. You will need 2 pieces of cling film that criss-cross.

14. Put one cake back into one of the tins, sponge finger side up. The cake won't be snug, as it will have shrunk while baking. Dust half the cocoa powder over the top of the cake. Spoon on all the mascarpone cream and make sure it is levelled off completely, using a spatula.

15. Now add the second cake, sponge finger side up. Make sure to press the cake down slightly so that all the layers meld together.

16. Place a circle of baking paper on top, wrap in the cling film, and chill until it's time to serve.

17. Just before you are ready to serve, dust the top of the cake with the remainder of the cocoa powder. Serve straight away.

ETON MESS CHEESECAKE

Serves 10–12

Though I love a baked cheesecake, I also love the ease of a cheesecake that sets in the fridge. Since the cake itself is simple to make, it gives me lots more time for creating decorations, like the beautiful meringue kisses and dehydrated strawberries that jazz up the top of this one.

1. Lightly grease a loose-bottomed 23cm round cake tin and line with baking paper.

2. Put the crushed biscuits in a bowl with the melted butter. Mix till it resembles wet sand. Empty into the cake tin and pack tightly with the back of a spoon, then place in the fridge for 15 minutes.

3. Whip the cream to soft peaks with the icing sugar and vanilla. Put the cream cheese into another bowl and stir to slacken.

4. Add the cream mix to the cream cheese, along with the strawberries, and fold together gently. Add to the chilled base and level off. Chill in the fridge while you prepare everything else.

5. To make the strawberry sauce, put the strawberries, icing sugar and lemon juice into a mixer and pulse to a purée. Transfer to a bowl and set aside in the fridge.

6. For the meringues, preheat the oven to 120°C/100°C/gas ½ and line a baking tray with baking paper. Fit a piping bag with a 1.5cm star tip nozzle and turn inside out. Stand it in a tall glass or jug.

7. Put the egg whites in a clean bowl and whisk. After 2 minutes they should be frothy and increased in volume. Gradually add the sugar, a little at a time, whisking constantly to form stiff peaks.

8. Using a brush and red food colouring, paint the inside of the piping bag with stripes, starting at the tip and painting up as far as you will fill the bag. Fill the bag with the meringue mix and pipe little kisses on to the tray. Bake for 1 hour, then turn off the oven, open the door and leave the meringues inside for another hour.

9. Remove the meringues from their tray and turn the baking paper over. Holding the strawberries by the stalk, dip them three-quarters of the way into the white chocolate. Place on the tray to set – you can put the tray in the fridge to speed this up.

10. Remove the cheesecake from the fridge, take out of the tin, and place on a presentation plate or stand. Decorate just before serving: pour over enough sauce to just cover the top (you may not need it all), and top with chocolate strawberries, mini meringues and lustred dehydrated strawberry slices.

PREP 1 HOUR, PLUS CHILLING
COOK 1 HOUR, PLUS COOLING

For the cheesecake
250g digestive biscuits, crushed

100g unsalted butter, melted

300ml double cream

100g icing sugar

1 tablespoon vanilla bean paste

600g full-fat cream cheese

18g freeze-dried strawberry pieces

For the sauce
200g strawberries, hulled

15g icing sugar

1 teaspoon lemon juice

For the mini meringues
50g egg whites (from 1–2 large eggs)

100g caster sugar

red gel food colouring

For the decoration
15 strawberries, whole

100g white chocolate, melted

10 dehydrated strawberry slices, sprayed with gold lustre (optional)

Photos overleaf →

COCONUT & BLUEBERRY TARTS
Makes 12

Any baking enthusiasts out there will know it takes time, effort and a whole lot of love to make 12 individual tarts. While it can be fiddly lining the tins with pastry, I promise you it's worth the trouble, not least for the 'oohs' and 'aahs' of your recipients when they see all the effort you've gone to. This creamy, coconutty filling works so well with the tart fresh blueberries. You'll need 12 tartlet tins, about 10cm in diameter, for this recipe.

**PREP 1 HOUR, PLUS CHILLING
COOK 40 MINUTES,
PLUS COOLING**

For the pastry
350g plain flour, plus extra
for dusting

175g unsalted butter, cubed

125g caster sugar

1 large egg, plus 1 extra
egg yolk

1 egg yolk, for egg wash

For the coconut cream
500ml whole milk

6 large egg yolks

120g caster sugar

50g cornflour

75g desiccated coconut

For the topping
300g fresh blueberries

40g toasted coconut chips

2 tablespoons icing sugar,
for dusting

1. Put the flour and butter into a food processor and blitz until the mixture resembles breadcrumbs.

2. Add the sugar, the whole egg and the extra egg yolk and blitz again until the dough turns into a clump. At this point stop the machine, otherwise the dough will become tough. Take out the dough, flatten and chill in the fridge for 1 hour.

3. Meanwhile make the coconut cream. Heat the milk in a pan until it just reaches a simmer, then turn off the heat. Put the egg yolks, caster sugar and cornflour into a bowl and whisk to combine.

4. Gently pour the warm milk into the egg mixture in a steady stream, whisking all the time. Once all the milk has been used, pour the mixture back into the pan and whisk on a low heat until it thickens enough that it will not run off a spoon. Take off the heat, stir in the coconut, then transfer to a bowl to cool.

5. Take the pastry out of the fridge and lightly dust the worktop with flour. Roll the pastry as thinly as possible, about 3mm. Using a tartlet tin as a guide, cut out circles to fit the tins with a little bit of overhang. Press the pastry into the tins and prick each base a few times with a fork.

6. Place a small square of greaseproof paper in each tin, on top of the pastry. Fill with baking beans and place all the tins in the fridge for 30 minutes.

7. Preheat the oven to 190°C/170°C fan/gas 5. Place the tins on baking trays and bake for 15 minutes, then take out of the oven and remove the paper and beans.

8. Brush inside each pastry shell with beaten egg yolk and put back in the oven for 5 minutes. Leave to cool in the tins for 15 minutes.

9. Carefully cut off the excess pastry from around the edges and take the cases out of the tins. Leave on a wire rack to cool completely then fill each tartlet case with coconut cream, top with blueberries and coconut chips, and dust with icing sugar.

JAFFA BAVAROIS

—————— *Serves 12* ——————

Are they cakes or are they biscuits? Should they be dunked or should they not? Can you eat them with a spoon? Well now you can, because this is my interpretation of the famous Jaffa combination, with light cake, zesty orange jelly and whipped chocolate, combined into a pudding version of the classic treat, just to add to the confusion of how it's 'supposed' to be eaten. I say that if something can't be answered, you might as well keep adding more questions.

1. This has a few stages, all quite simple, but let's begin with the jelly. First, soak the gelatine leaves in a bowl of cold water.

2. Place the orange juice in a small pan and bring to a gentle simmer (not a boil), then turn off and take off the heat.

3. Squeeze the excess water out of the gelatine, add it to the orange juice in the pan and mix to allow it to dissolve. (If you did accidentally bring the juice to a boil, wait for it to cool before adding the gelatine. Boiling liquids can make gelatine much less effective.)

4. Place the mixture in a shallow bowl or container and place in the fridge to set.

5. Now to get started on the bavarois cream. Put the gelatine leaves into a bowl of cold water and set aside.

6. Put the milk into a pan and just bring to a simmer, then take it off the heat.

7. Whisk together the eggs and sugar in a bowl. Slowly add the warm milk in a steady stream, until you have added it all.

8. Now pour the mixture back into the pan and place on a very low heat. The lowest setting you have is best. Stir continually until the mixture is thicker and coats the back of the spoon. Don't be tempted to speed up the process by turning up the heat, or the mixture will curdle. This is the perfect opportunity to catch up on social media, news or family with your free hand. The whole process can take 20–25 minutes.

9. Once the mixture has thickened, put it back into the bowl and leave for 10 minutes, just to cool. Add the gelatine and mix through. Put into the fridge and leave to cool completely.

10. Once the mixture is cold, whip the cream to soft peaks and fold into the egg mixture, making sure any lumps have gone. Add the orange zest, then put into the fridge.

Recipe continues overleaf →

**PREP 1 HOUR, PLUS CHILLING
COOK 40 MINUTES**

For the jelly
3½ gelatine leaves
300ml orange juice

For the bavarois cream
flavourless oil, for greasing
9 gelatine leaves
600ml milk
4 egg yolks
100g caster sugar
300ml double cream
zest of 1 orange

For the Genoese sponge
125g caster sugar
3 medium eggs
125g plain flour, sifted

**For the whipped
chocolate topping**
40g full-fat cream cheese
50g full-fat mascarpone
cheese
1 tablespoon whole milk
180g icing sugar, sifted
20g cocoa, sifted

11. For the Genoese sponge, preheat the oven to 200°C/180°C fan/gas 6. Line the sides and base of a deep 24 x 30cm rectangular baking tin with baking paper, leaving a bit of an overhang.

12. Whisk the eggs and sugar for 8–10 minutes, until the mixture is light and three times its original volume. When the whisk is swirled and lifted out, a trail should remain in the mixture for longer than 8 seconds. Add the sifted flour to the mixture and fold through carefully, making sure to get rid of all the pockets of flour without knocking out too much air.

13. Pour the mixture into the baking tin, then, using a spatula or the back of a spoon, spread it into the corners to make an even layer. Bake in the oven for 8–10 minutes, until the sponge is very light golden and slightly risen.

14. Once baked, remove from the oven. Take the sponge out of the tray, using the paper to help you, and leave to cool on a wire rack.

15. As the sponge cools, grease the same baking tin and line the base and sides generously with cling film. Grease lightly.

16. Chop up the orange jelly into small cubes and sprinkle them all over the base of the tray.

17. Pour over the bavarois cream, then put the Genoese sponge on top. The sponge will be slightly smaller now, as it will have shrunk during baking. But this is absolutely fine. Place in the fridge to chill for at least 3 hours.

18. While it chills, you can get started making the whipped chocolate topping. Put the cream cheese and mascarpone into a bowl with the milk and mix together so they are well combined and viscous. Add the sifted icing sugar and cocoa and mix through. Whisk for 2 minutes.

19. Take the bavarois out of the fridge and tip it over so the sponge is on the base and the bavarois on top. Cut into portions.

20. Place the chocolate cream in a piping bag with a star tip attached, and pipe out one large chocolate star for each portion.

PEAR & GINGER TRIFLE

Serves 8–10

Normally I'm not a massive fan of trifle. I have issues with that place where the cake meets the jelly and creates this weird cake–jelly hybrid that doesn't sit very well in my mouth. So this is my slightly upside-down version of the classic, with pear and ginger sitting in coconut jelly. It's topped with sticky ginger cake, custard and cream.

1. Place the leaves of gelatine in a bowl of cold water. Pour the coconut water into a small pan and heat up gently. Take off before it boils – you just want to warm it through.

2. Squeeze the excess water out of the gelatine sheets and add them to the coconut water. Stir until the gelatine has dissolved, then add the grated stem ginger and the ginger syrup.

3. You need a high 23cm wide dish for this. I like to use a glass trifle dish so I can see the layers.

4. Put the pears into the base of the dish and add half the coconut mixture. Place in the fridge and leave for 30 minutes, to set completely. This will allow the fruit to sit on the base instead of being suspended at the top of the jelly.

5. Now add the rest of the jelly and put back into the fridge to set. This should take about 2 hours.

6. Meanwhile, make your custard. Put the milk into a pan and heat until it just comes to the boil, then remove from the heat.

7. Mix the egg yolks, cornflour, sugar and vanilla paste and whisk until the mixture is light and fluffy. Slowly pour in the warm milk, making sure you're whisking all the time. Once you have added all the milk, put the mixture back into the warm pan and stir gently on a low to medium heat until it has thickened. Take off the heat and allow the custard to cool completely – it needs about 30 minutes in the fridge.

8. Put the chunks of ginger cake on top of the jelly mixture. Make sure the cake touches the edges of the dish so you can see a distinct cake layer.

9. Now spoon the chilled custard on top and smooth it out. Whip the cream, icing sugar and cornflour to soft peaks and dollop on top of the trifle, making peaks using the back of a knife.

10. Leave in the fridge until ready to serve.

PREP 40 MINUTES,
PLUS SETTING
NO COOK

For the jelly
7 gelatine leaves

500ml coconut water

2 pieces of stem ginger in syrup, grated (plus, 3 tablespoons of the ginger syrup)

1 x 230g tin of pears, drained and cut into chunks

For the vanilla custard
500ml whole milk

2 large egg yolks

3 tablespoons cornflour

25g caster sugar

1 teaspoon vanilla bean paste

For the ginger cake
240g ginger cake, chopped into chunks

For the cream
300ml double cream

2 tablespoons icing sugar

1 teaspoon cornflour

RAINBOW CAKE

— *Serves 8–10* —

While I can't resist a barrage of colour on anything edible, I do sometimes wonder what artificial colourings do to our insides. So, much as I love decorating cakes with multicoloured layers of sugary neon fondant, I am also always on the lookout for clever ways of paring things back. Hidden inside this simple vanilla cake is a subtle rainbow-stripe filling that satisfies my urges for food colouring, while the adornment of fruit on top makes use of the shades that nature has so kindly given to us. While developing this recipe, I happened to be working with a very special Chris Martin lookalike, and I realized how not being able to eat lactose can hinder some people from getting stuck in. So I found a way to make this recipe lactose-free. This one is for you, Chris! It's all for you!

**PREP 1 HOUR,
PLUS CHILLING
COOK 30 MINUTES,
PLUS COOLING**

For the cake
250g vegetable fat

250g caster sugar

4 medium eggs

2 tablespoons vanilla extract

250g self-raising flour, sifted

½ teaspoon baking powder

For the meringue frosting
3 egg whites

200g caster sugar

250g vegetable fat

2 tablespoons vanilla bean paste

gel food colouring
(red, orange, yellow, green, blue, purple, pink)

1. Preheat the oven to 190°C/170°C fan/gas 5. Grease the base of two 20cm round cake tins and line with baking paper.

2. Put the vegetable fat, sugar, eggs, vanilla extract, flour and baking powder into the bowl of a mixer, or use a hand-held mixer, and beat on high for 2 minutes, until you have a smooth and even cake batter.

3. Divide the mixture equally between the two prepared tins, and level off the top.

4. Bake in the oven on the middle shelf for 25–30 minutes, until the cakes are a light golden colour and coming away from the tin at the sides. A skewer inserted should come out clean.

5. Leave in the tin for 10 minutes, then turn out on to a wire rack and leave until completely cold.

6. Meanwhile, make the meringue frosting. Place a medium pan on the heat and add about 2½cm of water. Bring the water to the boil, then leave on a low gentle simmer.

7. Find a heatproof bowl that sits comfortably on top of the pan without moving too much. Put the egg whites and sugar into the bowl.

Recipe and ingredients continue overleaf →

4 strawberries, halved

1 clementine, peeled and segmented

8 dried apricots

8 green grapes

4 purple grapes

10 blueberries

8. With the bowl on top of the pan, begin to whisk with a hand-held mixer on medium speed. The mixture needs to come up to 60°C. If you don't have a cooking thermometer, test by taking a bit of the meringue and pressing the mixture between your fingers. Once you can't feel any sugar granules, the sugar has melted and the mixture is ready.

9. Take the pan off the heat and keep whisking. Add chunks of the vegetable fat and keep whisking. The mixture will begin to look runny and will then come together and look a lot more like buttercream.

10. Add the vanilla bean paste and whisk it in. The mixture is ready to use straight away.

11. Paint stripes of colour all around the inside of a piping bag, starting each stripe at the tip and working up to the top. Fill the piping bag with half the frosting mixture.

12. Pipe frosting on to the top of one of the cakes, starting from the outside and working your way in until you get to the centre. Place the other cake on top.

13. Using a spatula, place dollops of white frosting wherever you can see the coloured frosting, so as to conceal the rainbow surprise. Use the rest of the frosting to cover the whole top and sides of the cake. The mixture is airy, so you aren't looking for a smooth finish, but for one that's more textured.

14. Now decorate the top by placing the fruit around the edge.

WHITE CHOCOLATE &
GRAPEFRUIT TRUFFLES

Makes 25

Sometimes I prefer to serve up a dessert that doesn't need slicing or scooping or plates or washing up! So that's when I serve up truffles. After a particularly long or heavy meal, most grown-ups don't want to be faced with a big slab of pudding, and we would rather settle for a little something sweet with a cup of something hot. These white chocolate and grapefruit truffles are a favourite of mine for moments like this, as they are sweet with a distinctive sharpness.

1. Put the cream and butter into a pan and place on a medium heat. Just before the mixture comes to a simmer, take it off the heat and set aside.

2. Place the chocolate in a bowl and pour over the hot cream. Leave to sit for a few minutes, then mix. The chocolate should mix into the cream and the mixture should become viscous.

3. Add the grapefruit zest and vanilla paste.

4. Chill the mixture in the fridge until firm enough to roll. This may take a few hours.

5. When ready to shape the truffles, take a spoon, dip it into hot water and wipe off the moisture. Scoop up a small amount of the chocolate mixture (about 20g) and roll it in the palm of your hand. To stop the truffles sticking to your skin, you can lightly grease your hands with a flavourless oil.

6. Sift the icing sugar on to a large flat plate. Shape each truffle into a ball, then roll it in the icing sugar and press it into the back of an edible flower, flattening the truffle. This will ensure the flower stays stuck in the truffle.

7. Place the truffles in a sealed container in the fridge. Take out just before serving. They are best served the same day if you want the flowers to look their best.

PREP 25 MINUTES,
PLUS CHILLING
COOK 5 MINUTES

200ml double cream

50g unsalted butter

400g white chocolate,
chopped

zest of 1 yellow grapefruit

1 teaspoon vanilla bean paste

200g icing sugar

25 edible flowers

CARAMELIZED WHITE CHOCOLATE & HAZELNUT BUNDT CAKE

Serves 20

Discovering caramelized white chocolate was a revelation for me. At college I used to get a regular chocolate fix between lessons. Always rushing from one class to the next, I remember that fateful day at the vending machine when I pressed B4 instead of B1, and found myself with a Caramac bar, which I would never have chosen. I haven't looked back and caramelized white chocolate has been my favourite ever since, both to eat and to bake with. This cake is a lovely combination of sweetness and nuttiness, with a unique warmth from the toasted flour.

PREP 40 MINUTES
COOK 1 HOUR 15 MINUTES

For the cake

380g plain flour, plus extra for dusting

225g unsalted butter, softened, plus extra melted butter for greasing

500g caster sugar

4 medium eggs

120ml whole milk

1 tablespoon baking powder

1 teaspoon salt

100g roasted hazelnuts, roughly chopped

100g caramelized white chocolate, roughly chopped

For the topping

100g caramelized white chocolate, melted

25g roasted hazelnuts, roughly chopped

gold edible lustre dust

1. Put the flour into a large non-stick pan and toast over a medium heat, making sure to stir all the time. This should take about 10 minutes. The flour should be a golden brown colour. Take off the heat and set aside.

2. Preheat the oven to 180°C/160°C fan/gas 4. Brush the inside of a 23cm bundt tin with melted butter and dust it lightly with flour, gently tapping out any excess. Set aside.

3. Beat the butter and sugar in a mixing bowl until the mixture is light and fluffy and almost white in colour.

4. Add the eggs to the milk and whisk lightly. Slowly add the egg and milk mixture to the butter and sugar, making sure to incorporate it well.

5. Sift the flour into the bowl, along with the baking powder and salt. The flour will be in clumps after toasting, so be sure to use the back of your spoon to push the lumps through the sieve. Then fold in by hand, using a spatula or spoon. Add the hazelnuts and chocolate, and mix everything to a smooth batter.

6. Pour into the tin and level off the top. Bake on the middle shelf of the oven for 55 minutes to 1 hour, until a skewer inserted comes out clean and the cake is golden brown and slightly risen.

7. Leave to cool in the tin for 20 minutes, then turn out on to a wire rack to cool completely. If the cake is wonky when turned out, just slice the base so it is level and the cake will stand straight.

8. To decorate, gently spoon the melted chocolate over the cake. Alternatively, you could use a piping bag to do this.

9. Put the hazelnuts into a bowl with the gold lustre and mix until all the nuts are covered. Sprinkle all over the drizzled chocolate.

More photos overleaf →

ROCKY ROAD CAKE

Serves 16

I love the combination of chewy fruit, sticky marshmallow and crunchy biscuit, all covered in rich chocolate. Rocky road is one of the first things I ever made in the kitchen with the kids. I say 'made', even though it is more a case of 'putting together' as opposed to baking. But this variation is a rocky road with a soft landing – in cake form.

**PREP 45 MINUTES,
PLUS COOLING
COOK 1 HOUR 25 MINUTES**

For the cake

225g plain flour, sifted

350g caster sugar

85g cocoa powder

1½ teaspoons baking powder

1½ teaspoons bicarbonate of soda

250ml whole milk, room temperature

2 large eggs

125ml vegetable oil (or any flavourless oil)

250ml boiling water

2 tablespoons instant coffee

For the rocky road

250g dark chocolate, chopped

250g milk chocolate, chopped

100g unsalted butter

200g malted milk biscuits, roughly broken

100g marshmallows (if mini, that's great – if they are big they will need cutting into smaller pieces)

200g glacé cherries, halved

2 tablespoons icing sugar

1. Preheat the oven to 180°C/160°C fan/gas 4. Grease the base and sides of a 25cm round cake tin. Cut out two rounds of baking paper and use one to line the tin, putting the other one aside for later.

2. Put the flour, sugar, cocoa, baking powder and bicarbonate of soda into a large bowl and give it all a whisk.

3. Put the milk, eggs and oil into a jug and whisk until they are combined. Add to the dry mix and whisk to a smooth batter.

4. Using the same jug, measure out the boiling water and the coffee. Mix together and pour into the batter. You won't actually taste the coffee in the cake, but it enhances the flavour of the chocolate, so you should taste a lot of chocolate. This feels weird, and it seems the two will not mix together. But I promise that they will, so persevere and continue to mix until you get a smooth batter. But be careful – the water will be very hot.

5. Pour the batter into the prepared cake tin and bake on the middle shelf for 45–50 minutes, until a skewer inserted comes out clean. Leave to cool completely in the tin.

6. Meanwhile prepare the rocky road by putting the two chocolates and the butter into a microwaveable bowl and melting in the microwave until the mixture is smooth. Do this in 30-second and then 10-second bursts, stirring between bursts.

7. Now add the biscuits, marshmallows and glacé cherries, and mix well until everything is coated.

8. Pour the mixture all over the cooled cake, using the back of a spoon to help spread it out if needed. Now take the extra round of baking paper you cut out earlier, place it on top and press firmly to flatten. Place in the fridge for 2 hours.

9. Take the paper off the top and turn out on to a cake stand or serving plate.

10. Now take off the other piece of paper and dust the cake with icing sugar before slicing.

GINGERBREAD & LEMON VERTICAL CAKE

Serves 10

Ginger cake is my husband's absolute favourite, and yet in 12 years I can't remember ever having made a ginger cake specifically for him. He mentions this constantly, while conveniently forgetting all the other cakes I've baked him. So this is for Abdal, for his love of ginger, with lemon frosting, which just works. Its layers run vertically, which is a nice surprise when sliced.

PREP 45 MINUTES, PLUS CHILLING
COOK 1 HOUR 35 MINUTES

For the cake

230g golden syrup

115g light brown sugar

115g unsalted butter

275ml whole milk

1 large egg

225g self-raising flour, sifted

1 teaspoon bicarbonate of soda

2 tablespoons ground ginger, plus extra for sprinkling

55g stem ginger in syrup, washed, dried and finely grated

For the lemon cream cheese frosting

150g unsalted butter, very soft

150g full-fat cream cheese

600g icing sugar, sifted

zest of 2 lemons

1. Preheat the oven to 180°C/160°C fan/gas 4. Grease the base and sides of a 23cm square cake tin, and line with baking paper, making sure to leave a bit of an overhang.

2. Put the golden syrup, sugar and butter in a pan and warm until the butter has melted and the sugar dissolved. Set aside to cool.

3. Put the milk into a jug with the egg and whisk well.

4. Put the flour, bicarbonate of soda, ground ginger and stem ginger into a large bowl and mix together.

5. Now add the cooled golden syrup mixture from the pan and the milk mixture from the jug. Using a whisk, make sure the batter is lovely and smooth. It's a very loose mixture.

6. Pour into the tin and bake for about 1½ hours until the cake is shiny and golden and a skewer inserted comes out clean.

7. Leave to cool in the tin for 30 minutes, then remove, using the paper around the edge to help you, and cool on a wire rack.

8. Meanwhile, make the frosting by putting the butter and cream cheese into a bowl and mixing until smooth. Add the sifted icing sugar and mix again until combined and smooth.

9. Mix in the lemon zest and place the frosting in the fridge until you are ready to use it.

10. Once the cake has cooled completely, lay it on a board. Cut it down the centre, to give 2 equal rectangular pieces. Now cut each rectangle in half again lengthways, to create 4 long thin pieces.

11. Keeping the pieces on the board, nudge them far enough apart that you can get frosting into the gap between each layer. Fill each gap with frosting, then press the strips back together into their original square shape, but now with three stripes of frosting.

12. Finally, frost the sides and top of the cake and rib the edges using the tip of a spoon. Chill in the fridge for 30 minutes, until set.

BAKED VANILLA MOUSSE, MALT & HAZELNUT HONEYCOMB

Serves 6

I love mousse, but I wanted to create a version that didn't need gelatine. This is the outcome, which is set by being gently baked in the oven instead. Alone it's very simple, but it really comes into its own when drizzled with malt syrup and this easy-to-make hazelnut honeycomb.

1. Preheat the oven to 160°C/140°C fan/gas 3 and boil a full kettle of water. Grease four ramekins or dariole moulds of 8–9cm, and place a circle of greaseproof paper in the base of each one.

2. Beat the cream cheese and milk in a bowl until light and fluffy. Now add half the sugar, with the egg yolks, cornflour and lemon juice. Whisk until well combined and there are no more lumps.

3. Now whisk the egg whites in a separate bowl until they get foamy. Add the cream of tartar, then add the rest of the sugar slowly, whisking all the time. The mixture should be a stiff meringue, glossy and shiny.

4. Pour the meringue mix into the egg yolk mix and fold in gently. Add the vanilla extract. Mix and pour into the prepared ramekins.

5. Place the ramekins in a large roasting tin, then pour boiling water from the kettle into the tin to come halfway up the sides of the ramekins. Bake in the oven on a low shelf for 30–35 minutes. You will know they are ready when there is only a slight wobble left but the mixture has set.

6. Take out of the roasting tin and set aside until cool, then place in the fridge overnight.

7. To make the honeycomb, line a baking tray with baking paper. Place the sugar and syrup in a pan on a medium heat. Keep stirring – the mixture will become clear, runny and golden. You will know it's ready when all the sugar granules have dissolved.

8. Take off the heat and add the bicarbonate of soda. Mix quickly and pour on to the baking tray. Sprinkle immediately with hazelnuts and leave for up to an hour to set.

9. To serve, turn out each mousse pot on to a plate by just dipping it into hot water for a few seconds – this should loosen the whole thing without needing to put a knife around the edge. Drizzle over the malt extract, then break the honeycomb into shards and place the pieces on top.

**PREP 50 MINUTES,
PLUS OVERNIGHT COOLING
COOK 35 MINUTES**

For the mousse

butter or spray oil,
for greasing

200g full-fat cream cheese

60ml whole milk

120g caster sugar

3 large eggs, separated

20g cornflour

30ml lemon juice (approx.
1 lemon)

1 teaspoon cream of tartar

1 teaspoon vanilla extract

3 tablespoons malt extract

For the hazelnut honeycomb

200g caster sugar

5 tablespoons golden syrup

2 teaspoons bicarbonate
of soda

30g roasted hazelnuts,
chopped

ROSE & PISTACHIO DACQUOISE FLOWER

Serves 8–10

It took me longer to work how to pronounce 'dacquoise' than to actually make it! A dacquoise is essentially a meringue, but with crushed nuts folded through. Not too dissimilar to a macaron, but a lot easier. It's a light dessert that takes a bit of work, but the results are spectacular. Whether you have guests coming over or you are taking this to a friend's house, it's one of those creations where everyone can see you've made an effort. The fragrant combination of rose and pistachio adds even more wow factor.

1. Preheat the oven to 180°C/160°C fan/gas 4.

2. Put the pistachios into a food processor and blitz until they are coarsely ground. Place them in an even layer across a baking tray and place in the oven for 10–12 minutes, making sure to stir them every 3–4 minutes. The nuts need to be toasted and dried out.

3. Take the nuts out of the oven, put into a bowl and leave them to cool completely. Reduce the oven to 150°C/130°C fan/gas 2.

4. Once the nuts are cold, stir in 100g of sugar and the cornflour and set aside.

5. Line three baking trays with baking paper. Draw a 20cm circle on one piece. Now draw 4 lines across the circle so that they intersect in the middle, to divide the circle into 8 equal wedges – the way a cake would look if it was cut into 8 slices. Round off the edge of each wedge so that they are petal-shaped. Do the same on the other two pieces of paper, using the first as a template to trace over. Turn the paper over so it is pencil-side down.

6. Put the egg whites in a clean bowl and whisk for a few minutes, until frothy and increasing in volume. Now add the remaining 200g of sugar, a tablespoon at a time, still whisking, until you have used all the sugar. The mixture should now be stiff and glossy.

7. Add the pistachio mix to the meringue and fold it all in gently, making sure there are no dry nut bits.

8. Fit a piping bag with a plain 1.5cm nozzle and stand it inside a tall glass. Put the mixture into the piping bag and pipe the meringue inside the pencil lines, to fill in the flower shapes on all three trays.

Recipe continues overleaf →

PREP 1 HOUR, PLUS CHILLING
COOK 1½ HOURS

For the pistachio dacquoise
250g pistachios

300g caster sugar

25g cornflour

6 large egg whites

150g white chocolate, melted

For the rose custard
600ml whole milk

3 large egg yolks

125g caster sugar

2 tablespoons rose syrup

50g cornflour

300ml whipping cream

For decoration
40g crystallized rose petals, blitzed to coarse crumbs (see tip overleaf)

75g pistachios, blitzed to coarse crumbs

9. Place all three trays in the oven and bake for 1 hour, making sure to swap the top and bottom trays over halfway through, to ensure an even bake.

10. Once the hour is up, turn off the oven and open the door. Leave the meringues in the oven for at least an hour before taking them out. If you can wait longer, leave them until the oven is totally cold.

11. Meanwhile make the rose custard. Put the milk into a pan and bring to a simmer, then take off the heat and set aside. Put the egg yolks, sugar, rose syrup and cornflour into a bowl and whisk together. Slowly pour in the milk in a slow stream, making sure to whisk all the time. This is where you may need someone else to help.

12. Once all the milk is added, pour the mixture back into the pan on a low heat and bring to a simmer, whisking all the time. Then continue to whisk for 2–3 minutes, until it thickens. The custard needs to be thick enough to spread on the sides of the dacquoise.

13. Transfer to a bowl and leave to cool completely. Once cool, the custard will be quite thick, so you'll need to whisk it gently to loosen it just a little.

14. Once the rose custard is cooled, whip up the cream to soft peaks. Add half the whipped cream to the cooled custard and fold in. Then fold in the rest of the cream. Set aside in the fridge.

15. Meanwhile choose the best of your flower meringues and put it aside to make the top layer of the dacquoise. Brush the melted white chocolate over the tops of the other two meringues – the chocolate will stop the moisture from the rose custard seeping through.

16. Once the chocolate has set, it's time to assemble. Divide the rose custard into two batches, one for filling, one for covering the sides. Put the second batch aside.

17. Using the first batch, place one of the meringues on a serving dish, chocolate side up, and spread with a thin layer of the rose custard. Place the next chocolate-covered meringue on top and cover with more rose custard. Place the third and final meringue, the one you set aside, on top.

18. Using an angled spatula, cover the sides of the dacquoise with the second batch of rose custard. This will hide any imperfections. Take your time to make it all neat.

19. Now mix the blitzed rose petal and pistachio crumbs. Using your hands, press the crumb mixture all over the sides of the dacquoise.

Tip: To make homemade crystallized petals, brush organic rose petals (having made sure they are clean) with egg white, then cover them with caster sugar and leave them to dry.

Photo of the finished dacquoise overleaf →

CRISPY CHOCOLATE & SALTED PEANUT TART

Serves 10–12

This tart contains a surprising secret ingredient: crisps. Crisps have become such a snacking essential (one that I certainly couldn't do without) that most people don't think to use them in cooking. But with their crunchy, salty deliciousness, they are great added to recipes for extra texture and taste, and here I use crushed salted crisps to create a tart base with a difference. The chocolate filling is rich, but gets balanced out by the salty base and the scattering of salted peanuts. You will never look at crisps in the same way again – no longer just the crunch to accompany your sandwich, they can also be the crunch that accompanies your dessert!

PREP 25 MINUTES
COOK 45 MINUTES

For the base

250g thick-cut salted crisps

100g butter

4 tablespoons golden syrup

For the filling and topping

225g butter

375g dark chocolate (70% cocoa solids)

3 eggs

3 egg yolks

150g caster sugar

125g roasted and salted peanuts, roughly chopped

1. Preheat the oven to 180°C/160°C fan/gas 4, and grease a 23cm deep, loose-bottomed tart tin.

2. Whiz the crisps to breadcrumb-size pieces in a food processor. Melt the butter in a small pan with the golden syrup. Tip the crisps into a bowl and stir in the melted butter and syrup.

3. Press the crisp mixture evenly into the base and sides of the tart tin. Line the case with non-stick baking paper and fill with baking beans. Place on an oven tray and bake for 10 minutes. Remove from the oven, take out the paper and beans, and set aside.

4. Meanwhile make the filling. Melt the butter and chocolate in a heatproof bowl over a pan of gently simmering water (make sure the bottom of the bowl does not touch the water), stirring now and then until completely melted and glossy. Remove from the heat and leave to cool a little while you prepare the eggs.

5. Using an electric beater, whisk together the eggs, egg yolks and sugar till thickened and pale. This may take 3–4 minutes.

6. Pour the slightly cooled melted chocolate mixture over the egg and sugar mixture, whisking as you pour until completely combined. Stir in 75g of the chopped peanuts.

7. Pour the chocolate mixture into the tart shell and sprinkle the remaining chopped peanuts over the top.

8. Bake on the middle shelf of the oven for 20–25 minutes, or until almost set but still with a very slight wobble. If the tart is still very wobbly, cook for a little longer, but check it every couple of minutes. Remove and leave to cool on a rack, still in the tin. Then transfer to the fridge for at least 4 hours.

9. When cool, carefully remove the tart from the tin, cut into slices and serve with cream or vanilla ice cream.

INDEX

THANKS

Abdal, thank you for being the best human being in the world! I hope God made you out of some sort of hardwearing thermosetting material, because there should be more of you in the world. You are the most supportive husband a girl could ever ask for. I love you more than marmite crisps!

My babies – Musa, Dawud and Maryam – day by day you become more intuitive, kinder and lovelier than I could hope for. Every day spent away from you is tough, but each day spent with you is worth its weight in saffron.

Amma and Baba, for all of your struggles and for all the times you tried to convince me there was method to your madness. I believe you now. I get it!

Dhidhi, Sadiafa, Pinks, Jak and Shak. It's never about what we've done wrong, it's all about who gets in trouble with Mum first! From our first taste of milk, to our fights over the hand-washing bowl and our triumphant milk-drinking challenges. It all started with you guys.

Thank you to my agent Anne for being at the end of the phone every single day, at any hour. You are relentless in making sure I am always smiling – and not just on my face, but on the inside too. I don't know how you do it, but you do! It helps that you send me pictures of your shoes – that makes me happy in a way only you can truly understand.

To the television team! To the late nights, the long days and the many car trips. We got there in the end. Thank you to Paolo Proto, Stephen Leigh, Martha Delap, Laura Abrahams, Laia Niubo, Irina Aggrey, Becky Church, Nicole Larmour, Brendan Cornelissen, Pooch Horsburgh, Tom Kirkman and David Bimsom.

A special thank you to the man who knows my face better than anyone else. Danny Rohrer, you have the displeasure of looking at my face through a lens for hours on end! I would never have it any other way. I hope the sore shoulder was worth it for you. Thank you for tilting your head and reminding me that I can do it every time you see worry in my eyes. I can't thank you enough for being there for me.

For all the legends who've worked tirelessly to get this book in ship-shape order. Huge thank you to John Hamilton, Ione Walder, Dan Bunyard, Sarah Fraser, Claire Bush, Gaby Young, Chris Terry, Emma Lahaye, Rob Allison, Danny, Rosie McKean, Katy Gilhooly, Beatrix McIntyre, Amy McWalters, Annie Lee, Deborah Hooper and Caroline Wilding.

Heather B, you are a superstar. For every time you had to straddle me in order to make me look and feel a million dollars, it was worth it! You are an artist like I have never met. Thank you for making me feel amazing.

Thank you to all the people I visited while making this book and TV series. Thanks for letting us take over your lives for a day. Meeting people like you made the experience of writing recipes and filming the series all the more wholesome. I learned a lot about myself along the way, and got to see my Britain in a whole new light. I also learned the hard way that my legs were made for land and not for sea!

MICHAEL JOSEPH

UK | USA | Canada | Ireland | Australia
India | New Zealand | South Africa

Michael Joseph is part of the Penguin Random House group of companies
whose addresses can be found at global.penguinrandomhouse.com.

First published 2017
003

Colour reproduction by Altaimage Ltd
Printed in Italy by Printer Trento srl

A CIP catalogue record for this book is available from the British Library

ISBN: 978-0-718-18766-8

www.greenpenguin.co.uk

MIX
Paper from
responsible sources
FSC® C018179

Penguin Random House is committed to a
sustainable future for our business, our readers
and our planet. This book is made from Forest
Stewardship Council® certified paper.